Yachting

the golden age

Jean-Michel Barrault

Yachting
the golden age

HACHETTE
Illustrated

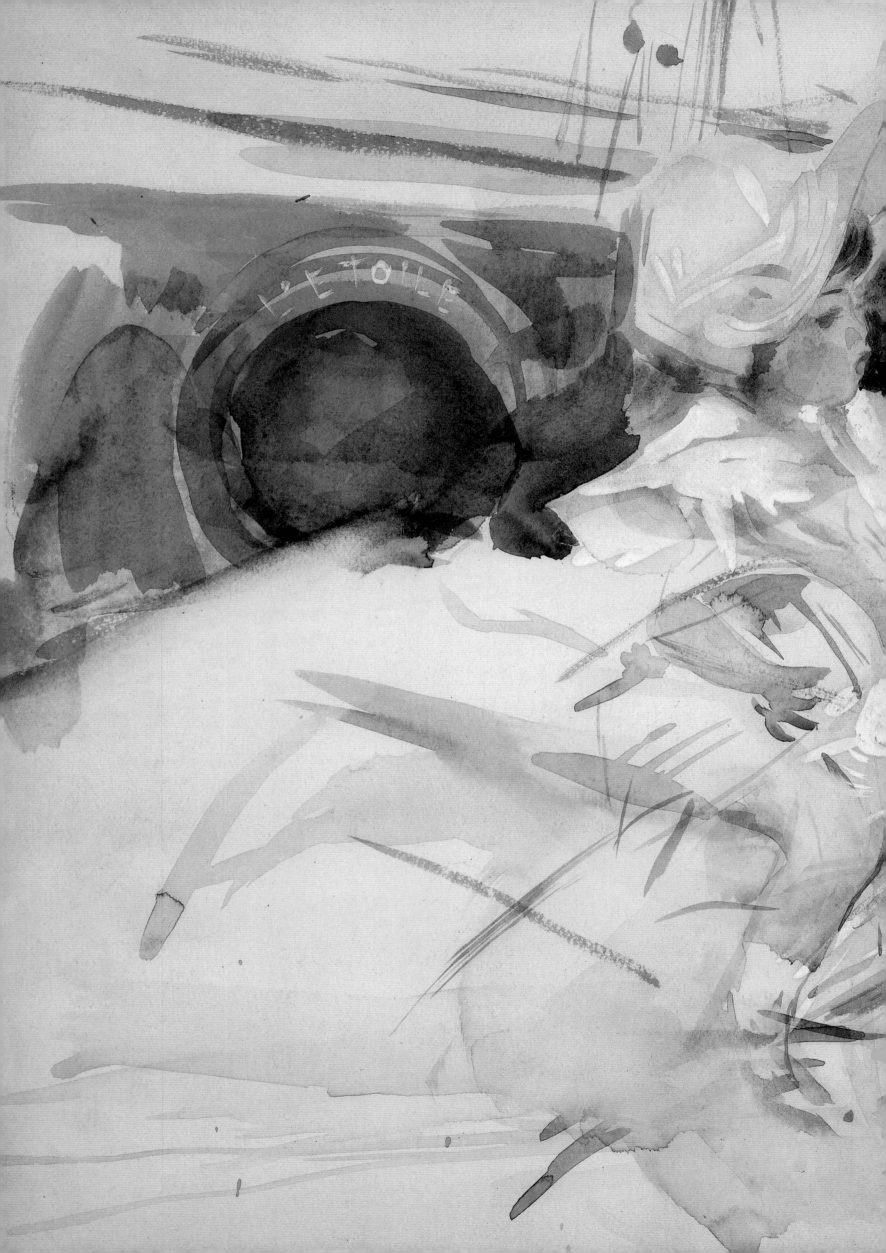

Contents

Royal yachting

The Kaiser was sailing at Kiel with the German and British war navies lined up as if on parade, anchored in single file they formed a guard of honour on each side of the course. Wilhelm II, dressed in the uniform of a naval officer was sailing on board the *Meteor IV* his 48-m (157-ft) schooner when a small steamboat suddenly turned towards the yacht at full speed, intent on coming alongside. The emperor, furious that someone should interrupt his sailing, ordered that the 'Do not board' signal be made. Admiral Muller then folded his message in a pack of cigarettes and threw it on board the yacht. When the Kaiser realised just how urgent the message was, he had to admit that he doubted anyone was going to be able to enjoy yachting for a while. The admiral had brought the sovereign news of the assassination at Sarajevo. For sailing, as for the world, the 1914–18 war marked the end of a golden age of half a century of peace and prosperity. Under Victoria's long reign as Empress of India, Great Britain ruled the world. The British flag flew proudly over all the countries of the Empire, India, Canada, Australia and New Zealand. As in the English sailors' song *Britannia rule the waves!* In the very young American nation, strong from her recent independence, a generation of bold multimillionaires was developing. They set out to conquer the West, building towns, railways, and roads, founding steelworks, shipping companies, factories and mine workings, sowing the vast, fertile plains of the Mid-West, finding gold in California and Alaska, encouraged by bankers and businessmen excited by the risks. In Europe, in the wake of the industrial revolution, businesses were set up and expanded. Among them were coal and iron mines, metal works, with energy created from the all-new electricity, textile factories, car plants, railways, the first planes and naval shipyards. The construction of buildings, too, particularly in Paris with the drastic re-arrangement of the capital ordered by Baron Haussmann, contributed to the enormous fortunes being made, especially as taxation was light and income tax still unknown in the majority of countries. There is no question that the workers who slaved away over 12-hour days, the peasants in the service of the large landowners or the employees of the new department stores paid a high price for this opulence. But at the same time, in Cowes, at Long Island and Newport, in the Mediterranean and on the Atlantic, the symbols of wealth of the few were being sailed. Superb schooners, racing cutters and steam yachts as fast as supremely refined liners, all contributed to the time that will always be thought of as the Golden Era of yachting.

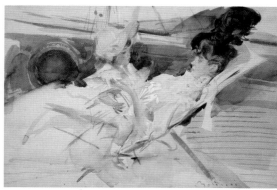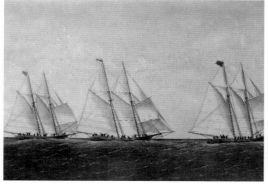

The yachtsmen who owned these pleasure boats were not only the owners of vast estates, captains of industry, entrepreneurs and bankers, but also members of the aristocracy and royal families, and those whose inheritance enabled them to live a life of leisure. Some were passionate about sailing but the majority of them succumbed to vanity, being content to exhibit these outward signs of wealth, never setting foot on board their sumptuous schooners or prestigious three-masters while some found the ease and attractions of cruising in large steam yachts.

This image of luxury yachting is still with us: men wearing white trousers, blue blazers, club ties, shirts with stiff collars and white caps; and women, when allowed on board, rivalling the men's elegance in immaculate long dresses of finely striped flannel, blouses with starched cuffs and collars, navy blue fitted coats and wide-brimmed hats or smart boaters. Parasols protected the ladies' delicate complexions. The yacht clubs laid down the evening dress the members had to wear when they joined. Braid stripes and stars signalled the hierarchy of committee officers. Distinctive markings on standards flown at mastheads gave the position of the owner, president, commodore, vice-commodore, general secretary... For an ordinary cruise, according to the experts, one had to take, in addition to sailing clothes, evening dress with shoes, an outfit for town, three linen shirts, several white ties, some gloves and six removable collars.

With rare exceptions, it was out of the question for these yachtsmen to take part in handling the boats. It was the responsibility of the sailors to run and maintain their boats; the captains and crews formed a professional cast of formidable competence. They were all in uniform: the captains in blue woollen cloth suits, with blue caps sometimes decorated with gold braid, and the sailors in woollen cloth tunics and trousers, blue wool polo neck shirts or sweaters embroidered with the name of the yacht and straw hats 'whose reflections lightened the faces and made a cheerful scene'. During the confrontations of these giants, which were 9 m (30 ft) to 12 m (40 ft) long, spectators flocked to the banks of the Solent, along the coasts of Long Island, and to yacht club terraces. People came, whether as connoisseurs, or simply to enjoy the free spectacle of the regattas, the men with bowler hats and walking sticks, the women in long dresses, with broad brimmed hats and parasols. Orchestras played on the lawns. The American historian, William P. Stephens noted ironically: 'numerous women in spring clothing were escorted by old beaux from the "rocking-chair fleet" too old or too blasé to take part'. They all had good reason to admire for in the latter part of the nineteenth century and at the beginning of the twentieth, at a cost of tens of thousands of pounds, dollars or francs to the elite few, privileged by birth or fortune, the most imposing, most sophisticated and most luxurious fleet of all time ruled the seas.

PAGES 4–5 AND CENTRE PAGE OPPOSITE
Yachtsmen left the running of their boats to their sailors. Here, on board Columbia *the crew are preparing to set the spinnaker.*

PAGES 6–7 AND OPPOSITE RIGHT
Satanita *and* Rainbow *in 1898.*

PAGES 8–9 AND CENTRE
Spectators flocked to watch the confrontations between the giants of the seas, as here, during the 1880 Cowes regatta.

PAGES 10–11 AND ABOVE LEFT
Madame Helleu and her daughter Paulette on their yacht, painting by Giovanni Boldini (1842–1931).

PAGES 12–13 AND ABOVE CENTRE
The American schooners Henrietta, Fleetwing *and* Vesta, *at the start of the 1866 transatlantic race, engraving by Charles Parsons.*

PAGE 14 AND ABOVE RIGHT
Yachting in the Edwardian era was characterised by the elegant refinement and financial ease of the British aristocracy, as shown here by Prince Alexander of Battenburg with his mother Beatrix of England on board Erin *in 1908.*

Britannia rules
the waves!

THE
ROYAL YACHT SQUADRON
WALTZES,

BLOODHOUND.

PANTOMIME.

R. Y. SQUADRON CASTLE.

COMPOSED
AND
ARRANGED
BY
T. H. BARNETT.

CETONIA.

EGERIA.

ENT. STA. HALL.

LONDON;
T. H. BARNETT, MUSIC PUBLISHER,
67, HIGH ST ST JOHNS WOOD, N.W.

Price 4/-

WILLEY & Cº 52. Gt MARLBOROUGH STREET, W.

The British are a nation of sailors. The first yacht club in the world was formed in Cork in Ireland as early as 1720. Its 25 members were entitled to wear a superb uniform and the club rules stated that 'each member will receive in turn'. The club was to disappear in 1765, but was reformed in the nineteenth century under the name of the Royal Cork Yacht Club. However, the Russians would argue that theirs was the first, as Peter the First founded the Neva Flotilla in 1718.

In England, the Cumberland fleet on

the Thames was the forerunner of the Royal Thames Yacht Club, but it was the Solent, that strip of water between the South Coast and the Isle of Wight, which very early on became the favourite playground of yachtsmen. One of the first races took place in 1815. It was between Joseph Weld's *Charlotte* and Thomas Ashleton-Martin's *Elizabeth*, two 65-ton cutters contesting a 500-guinea stake. That same year under the patronage of the Marquis of Anglesey, the Governor of the Isle of Wight, the most prestigious club in the world was founded at Cowes, and was given the title of Royal Yacht Squadron in 1833. This conferred on its members the privilege of flying a white flag on their yachts, carrying the coat of arms of the British Empire, the white ensign. Since 1540 two forts had stood on either side of the Medina River where yachts used to shelter. The fort on the west bank was the residence of the Marquis of Anglesey and it was only on his

death in 1857 that the club moved into the fort and converted it into a clubhouse. The terrace was furnished with brass canons and flagpoles used to signal the start of the races, and telescopes to follow the progress of the yachts. An immaculately kept lawn became the Mecca for receptions even though ladies were never admitted to the interior of the clubhouse.

From 1843, the young Queen Victoria, by then aged 24 and a sovereign for six years, ordered the construction of a 62-m (203-ft) yacht with paddle wheels, named *Victoria and Albert*. This forced the Royal Yacht Squadron, until then open only to sailing vessels, to accept this new type of boat. In 1845 the Queen bought Osborne House from Lady Isabella Birchford, a house built in the style of the Italian renaissance, and situated on the hill overlooking the east bank of the Medina River, and had it extended. For sea bathing the Queen used a bathing hut on wheels, which was rolled across the grass to the water's edge. Victoria soon found her yacht too small for her, her husband, her nine children and their attendants. *Victoria and Albert II*, launched in 1855 measured 82 m (269 ft). Still driven by paddle wheels to avoid the vibrations from a propeller, the new royal yacht reached speeds of up to 15 knots. The Prince Consort designed the majority of the furnishings predominantly in his favourite colour of green. The cabins were comfortable rather than luxurious, and Victoria preferred her own room with its deep sofa, upright piano and maps hung on the walls, to the large formal ceremonial saloon towards the stern, decorated with china pots. Even though she was ill in rough weather, Victoria liked to sail around the British Isles and the French coast preferring the Solent above all. Sheltering from an icy breeze one day, the Queen and two of her ladies-in-waiting had just sat down in the lee of one of the paddle wheels. The Sovereign noticed that

Under the patronage of the Marquis of Anglesey, the Governor of the Isle of Wight, the most prestigious club in the world was founded at Cowes in 1815, and given the title of Royal Yacht Squadron in 1833.

*The races took place in the Solent and around the Isle of Wight.
Many of the owners stayed ashore and watched their yachts
being raced by their paid crews.*

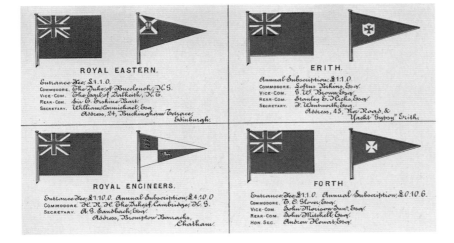

the sailors were whispering to each other.
She asked what they were talking about and
discovered that her deckchair was blocking
the way to the armoury where the grog rations
were stored. She agreed to move providing
that she could have a share of the ration, and
afterwards commented 'it would have been
better if it had been a little stronger'.

For the British gentry, the regattas in
the Solent were an obligatory part of elegant
society life. High society consisted for the most
part of owners of extensive estates, members of
the House of Lords and officials from the far
corners of the Empire who had been rewarded
with honours and gold. The nobility followed
an annual rite, a cycle which started with
presentation at the Court, followed by the
Derby and Ascot, and after the sailing season,
finished with grouse shooting. The activities of

the great racing yachts followed an immutable programme. Racing started in May on the Thames, and continued round to Dover. A Yankee yachtsman, Gerald B. Lambert, who had come to participate in the racing was surprised at the definition of the start line. 'The alignment of a lamp post on the jetty with the eastern face of St Mary's church tower. One had to know all about lamp posts and be familiar with ecclesiastical architecture!' The yachts continued in convoy to races that took place in the St George Canal, Liverpool, on the Clyde, in Ireland, and then returned to Falmouth and Plymouth to be back in Cowes for August. Each one hoped to pass the royal yacht and pay respects to the Sovereign. The races took place in the Solent and around the Isle of Wight. Many of the owners stayed ashore and watched their yachts being raced by their paid crews. When the owners were on board and their yachts met they would courteously salute each other by removing their hats, which in no way diminished their fervent battles, since the paid crews were keen to win the prizes for victory. The confrontations could even be so fierce that they led to boarding and sword fights.

There was no racing on Sundays, so then lords and ladies liked to take the air on the beach near their yachts. Most of the races took place in the afternoon, between lunch and dinner, and the day was rounded off with sumptuous evening receptions. Entry to the Royal Yacht Squadron was reserved to an aristocratic elite. Admission was by vote using black and white balls. If just one of the ten balls were black the candidate would be refused, which gave rise to the expression 'blackballed'. It was even said that a member would refuse to allow any applicant whose name began with the same letter as his so that he could just glance at the club's pigeonholes to see if they contained any of his mail. However, the club did admit such rich industrialists as Edward Guinness, the king of beer, who later became Lord Iveagh, or Richard Hennessy, the prince of Cognac.
Sir Walter Raleigh wasn't afraid of criticising the activities of these sportsmen. 'The so-called yachtsmen at Cowes lunch on champagne in the Solent, then they unfurl their canvas and go sailing for two hours if the wind is favourable and light. The people they meet at Cowes are much the same as those they meet at grouse

ABOVE
With Queen Victoria staying on the Isle of Wight, Cowes Week was the obligatory meeting place for the British gentry who crowded onto the terraces at Cowes to watch the races, painting by John Strickland Goodall (1909–1996).

FACING PAGE, BELOW
The yacht club flags were recorded in Lloyd's Register of Shipping.

shoots, and their life which may look idyllic, could also be a type of hell. The clothes may be different, but the bodies are equally well fed and carefully maintained by physical exercise, they all have the same jaded spirits, tired of wondering if anything exciting could ever happen'. They walked up and down the High Street, visited Astkey, the yacht chandler,

Ratsey's sail-loft, and at the top of the town the office of Frank Beken, the pharmacist, who took such wonderful photographs of yachts. Another commentator went even further: 'The same people always meet in the same little houses and at the same villas, the same rattan armchairs are enthroned on the club lawns welcoming the same people, pillars of society

in this town for years on end. They greet each other like old friends and an external observer would feel as if he was intruding on a family reunion'. These regulars held conversations between themselves that were full of unintelligible allusions for the uninitiated and which formed an unbridgeable barrier for them. As Mrs Nicholas Mathews Condy said with a sigh: 'it is pleasant enough to spend a week at Cowes as long as it is the sailing week and you can go out every day into lively surroundings. We have been as pleased with sailing around the island as by the champagne lunches, the really enjoyable archery contest at Carisbrooke and, to crown it all the amazingly brilliant Royal Yacht Squadron Ball'. Thomas Fleming Day, chief editor of *The Rudder* magazine, doubtless speaking out of jealousy, added 'those miserable carcasses who spend their days knocking back alcohol on the club terraces and who, if they have travelled a few miles in a 10-knot breeze, think they have had the time of their lives'. Lord Cardigan, on being invited on board a yacht, was asked whether he would like to take the helm. 'No, thank you, I never take anything between meals'. One owner who took a famous naval architect on board was rebuked for having consorted with someone from a lower class. It was easy for the columnists, ordinary people frustrated by not

belonging to the restricted circle of the great and the good, to make ironic comments. It was also unjust since many of the followers were passionate and able amateurs.

Lord Brassey, who had travelled around the world with his wife and children, was one of these. A Member of Parliament and the Liberal Party, this gentleman benefited from the large fortune amassed by his father, one of the principal builders of the British railways. In 1874 he built *Sunbeam*, a 52-m (170-ft) three-master, with 770 m² (8,828 ft²) of sail and fitted with a 350-horsepower auxiliary engine which gave her a top speed of 8 knots. *Sunbeam* proved to be a good sailing ship and in 1905 the schooner took part in the Kaiser's Atlantic race. For Lord Brassey, 'although fashion is turning strongly towards steam ships, the beauty of white sails and the gentle progress of a boat under sail will fascinate travellers for a long time. It is pleasant to be free of the rumbling of machines, the smell of oil, and the horrors of the inevitable coal'. Lady Brassey, who shared her husband's taste in travel was to be the first yachtswoman to sail around the world. She was a dark-haired, beautiful lady with dazzling white teeth, a yachtswoman who charmed all her contemporaries. 'One of those elite creatures who would shine wherever fate

collar. Between Honolulu and Yokohama, *Sunbeam* ran into two fierce storms. 'Thank God the children weren't frightened,' Lady Brassey said gratefully. There was a fire, caused by the sparks from the chimney, which was put out only with difficulty. The yacht returned home via Hong Kong and the Red Sea on 27 May 1877, less than ten months after she left. More than half the world tour was accomplished under sail with a daily record journey time of 299 miles. Lady Brassey's written account in which the yachtswoman evoked her love of boats was sold in large numbers: 'if you pass downwind of one of these yachts you will smell the combined scents of fresh varnish, of linseed oil, of the cream for polishing brass, of Havana cigars and of champagne, all mixed with the light scent of teak and other exotic woods'. In 1886, the Brasseys set out on a second circumnavigation. Lady Brassey, suffering from malaria, died off the coast of Australia and was buried at sea at 15°50 South and 110°38 East.

Lord and Lady Brassey set sail
on their world tour with their four
children, a doctor, five guests, two dogs,
three birds and a Persian cat on board.

This luxurious and prosperous
existence would have continued perfectly untroubled, if it were not for the disturbance caused by an intruder in 1841. As far as the English were concerned the United States of America was their former colony, which in 1776 had dared to win its independence after a victorious war against the British troops and the Navy. The gentry thought that this young nation was mainly inhabited by poor immigrants among whom were some who were the *nouveaux riches* and almost not to be associated with. And some of them had had the sheer audacity to build a schooner, call it *America* and then have the impudence to claim that they could beat the best yachts in the Solent, and on their home water. The challenge made by Commodore Stevens, the president and founder of New York Yacht Club caused some amazement in the small world of British sailing. They made fun of the boast. In 1849, the Marquis of Anglesey on his boat *Pearl* had lost a race to the Bermudas by just 55 seconds. His cutter was more than 30 years old as against the American yacht, which was newly out of the boatyard.

On 8 August 1851, when *America* arrived in the Solent and anchored to wait for a wind, *Laverock* an English sailing boat went to meet her. Stevens' pride led him to commit the sin of making a tactical error. When the wind came up, *America's* team trimmed the sails and demonstrated the cutter's superiority so well that the British yachtsmen politely declined all the offers of a meeting proposed by John Stevens. It was only on 22 August that the strangely rigged cutter was allowed to face the best of the British fleet in the traditional race around the Isle of Wight. Rumours and articles written in *The Times* transformed this contest into an event. Crowds gathered, from Portsmouth and Southampton on paddle

takes her, whether behind a milliner's counter, in charge of a primary school, or at the helm of a steam yacht' (Philippe Daryl, *Le Yacht*).
On 21 July 1876, *Sunbeam* set off on her journey round the world. There were 43 people on board, the Brasseys and their four children, a doctor, five guests, servants, the captain, the crew, two dogs, three birds and a Persian cat because the Brasseys were extremely fond of animals. The trip began in Rio. In the Magellan Straits, an English cargo boat was on fire and its crew of 15 were picked up by the *Sunbeam*. They continued on their way to Tahiti and Honolulu. When they crossed the equator, it was so hot that Sir Thomas went so far as to take off his jacket, his waistcoat and his stiff

steamers. One could hardly walk along the High Street, Cowes' narrow main road lined with houses. People were crowded on the terraces and the shore. It was a standing start and due to some clumsy handling, *America* started in last place to the amusement of the experts watching through their binoculars and telescopes. *America* wasn't long in catching up with her competitors who tried to prevent her from overtaking. John Rutherford, who was on board *America*, said: 'we caught up with a large yacht by the buoy at No Man's Land. Dick Brown (*America's* captain) tried to go past upwind but the others soon luffed us. The skipper pulled the helm to go to leeward. The other yacht quickly bore away to cover them. Somewhat annoyed by this tricky manoeuvre, "Old Dick" asked his boss. "Commodore, can I knock his block off with my bowsprit?" Stevens. "No, don't do that!" Then he turned to the member of the RYS, who was a Royal Navy captain as well. "Captain, you may call that fair play on this side of the ocean, but on our side we would call it a crude foul"'. Once around the eastern tip of the island, the American schooner was in the lead. Her main competitors were in difficulties. *Wyvern* had problems and had to turn back, *Arrow* went aground, *Alarm* came to her aid and then escorted her to Cowes,

Freak and *Volante* collided and *Volante* with her bow-sprit smashed, abandoned the race. However a small cutter, Thomas Le Marchant's *Aurora* was catching *America* up. She wasn't more than ten minutes behind at St Catherine's Point, the southernmost tip of the island, but then the best speed was to be made offshore in the schooner's favour.

Queen Victoria's steam yacht was anchored off the Needles. Her children, among them Edward who was then 10 years old, had returned to land because of the mist but were in time to see the schooner go past. *America* rounded the point at 5.50 p.m. The American yacht courteously dipped her flag three times to salute the royal yacht. Stevens, his guests, and all the crew doffed their hats. The wind dropped, the ebb tide was against them. *Victoria and Albert* with the Queen on board accompanied the schooner for a short while, then *America* was ordered to go ahead while *Victoria and Albert* anchored near the finishing line. Most of the spectator boats, with the journalists on board, followed the steamer. *America* crossed the line at 8.37 p.m.

The victory was greeted with astonishment. No one took any notice of the second, much smaller boat *Aurora*, scarcely a few hundred metres behind the victor and finishing only eight minutes later, and who would have easily

PRECEDING DOUBLE PAGE
In 1876–1877 Lord and Lady Brassey cruised round the world on board Sunbeam *their 52-m (170-ft), three-masted schooner (lithograph from the Brassey family collection, published in the 1907 edition of* British Yachts and Yachtsmen).

FACING PAGE, TOP
An idle moment on the deck of the Sunbeam.

FACING PAGE, BELOW
Lord and Lady Brassey. Lady Brassey died at sea during their second world cruise. In her account of the journey, she wrote, 'Thank God the children weren't frightened'.

ABOVE
Lady Brassey's cabin on board Sunbeam.

ABOVE
British pride suffered a terrible blow in 1851 when an American schooner, America, *beat the best English yachts in their own waters.*

FACING PAGE, TOP
Sir Richard Hutton's Genesta *didn't manage to win back the America's Cup in 1885, but her owner won a flattering reputation for fair play and sportsmanship.*

FACING PAGE
William Fife junior (centre) and G. L. Watson (below) Despite all their skill as architects, their designs never managed to defeat the best American yachts.

FOLLOWING DOUBLE PAGE
Britannia, a 35-m (115-ft) cutter, designed by George Watson for the Prince of Wales, racing Westward, *the 41-m (134.5-ft) American schooner designed by Nat Herreshoff.*

won on handicap. *Wildfire's* performance was also ignored. This Irish cutter, less than 20 m (60 ft) in length, was not allowed to join the race as she had moveable ballast that her crew shifted on each tack. She started after the fleet, but arrived at Cowes long before *America*. It didn't matter! A legend was in the making and the American victory was seen as a wound in the side of the proud British lion, and gave a lie to the emblematic song *Britannia rule the waves!*

On the day after her victory *America* anchored close to the shore at Osborne Bay. Queen Victoria and Prince Albert were conducted aboard *America* and received with full formality by Commodore Stevens. As Albert started down the gangplank, the captain, Dick Brown, told him to wipe his feet. The Prince Consort, taken aback, started and eyed the impertinent captain scornfully from head to toe, but the captain kept calm and replied 'I know who you are, but you have to wipe your feet all the same'. After a heated debate in the House of Commons, everyone in England thought that it was important to avenge this insult and regain the 100-guinea cup won by this New York Yacht Club which had only just been in existence for seven years! This preoccupation was to dominate British yachting throughout the Edwardian era.

America's superiority did not dull the enthusiasm of British yachtsmen. There were 45 yacht clubs in 1875, and the number of names on the register of yachts increased from 320 to 1,000 in the space of six years. *Bloodhound* built by Fife in 1874 for the Marquis of Ailsa, was all set for a long and brilliant career. This 19-m (62-ft) cutter with a straight bow was unluckily sunk by a steam yacht on the start line. But it was to be re-floated, then burnt in 1922. The mast survived and is now the Royal Yacht Squadron's flagpole. The era of large schooners of 30 m (98 ft) overall length began in 1860 and there were more than 30 of them racing. *Egeria* was the fastest of her time compared with *Titanic*, *Gloriana* and *Cambria*.

This was also the time of rivalry between two great Scottish architects, the Fifes who were a dynasty of designers, and George Watson, who was the son of a physician and was born in Glasgow in 1851, the year of *America's* victory. An American cutter, *Sappho*, which had come to sail in British waters was beaten in 1868 thereby proving that the American yachts were not invincible after all. Two years later, James Ashbury the owner of *Cambria* was the first to try his luck. His father had become very wealthy by inventing a system of grouping the multiple wheels under wagons. James had

inherited his father's fortune but was still treated with disdain by British nobility and he issued his challenge on behalf of the Royal Thames Yacht Club, and not of the Squadron since they had turned down his membership application. After *Cambria*'s defeat he issued a second, just as unsuccessful, challenge in 1871 with a new yacht the *Livonia*.

In 1873, George Watson, only just 22 years old, opened an office in Glasgow and wrote to British yatchsmen. He wanted to start a new career as a designer of racing and steam yachts. Moreover because of his family background, he would be the first to design his hulls using a scientific approach. Up until then yards were building according to tradition, at best constructing scale models which were used as a guide for the lines of the proposed boat. In 1881 Watson had designed *Madge*, a cutter with an overall length of 14 m (46 ft), for a well known Scottish yachtsman, James Coats. It was a pretty sailing boat in the British tradition, with a straight bow, black hull, white deck, and was managed by James Duggan, a well known professional, and a perfectly trained crew. *Madge* was sent to the United States where, except in very light winds, she beat all the similar-sized yachts she came up against. The British cutter's design was different to that of *Scheme* her main adversary. With a length of 14 m (46 ft), *Madge*'s maximum beam was 2.7 m (7.9 ft), her ballast 10.5 tonne (23,148 lb). *Scheme* was 13.5 m (39.8 ft) long, 4.2 m (14 ft) wide, carried only 4.5 tonne (9,920 lb) of ballast and had a centreboard for sailing close to the wind. *Madge*'s success was encouraging. In 1885, *Genesta*, an English cutter, won all the trials in her home waters. Her owner's challenge rightly worried the Americans who deployed all their designers' and sailors' skills to repel this assault. Sir Richard Sutton showed a fine example of fair play and sportsmanship.

A little after the start of the first race on 8 December 1885, the American defender, *Puritan*, collided with *Genesta* and was disqualified. Normally the British cutter would have been declared the winner, but her owner turned down such a victory, and asked for the race to be re-run. He lost that race and all the ones that followed. The *Galatea* was no more successful, and the era of the schooners was followed by the supremacy of the giant cutters. In 1887, James Bell issued his challenge in the name of the Royal Yacht Club. The agreement between the two clubs stated that both the challenger and the defender must measure 26 m (85 ft) at the waterline. Naturally the responsibility of designing the British challenger fell to the fashionable designer, George Watson. *Thistle* was designed in the greatest secrecy and built of Martin steel by the shipyard of D. & W. Henderson. From the start of its construction the hull was hidden under tarpaulins but as soon as she was on the water *Thistle*'s speed was revealed, and she won 11 out of her 15 races. When she arrived in the United States she looked like a scarecrow, but she was beaten as the surface area of her keel meant she was not as good upwind as the American boat. George Watson explained that the *Thistle* had been developed from a scientific process, and that the science wasn't yet certain enough, but that success was secondary. He said that in mechanically based sports there was often more engineering in failure than in success, since a good idea rarely died but would lead on to a new design. The result of his theory was to be seen very quickly in two exceptional yachts, the *Valkyrie II* and *Britannia*.

In 1889 and 1890, there was fierce competition in British waters between *Irex*, *Thistle*, *Yarama*, *Iverna* and the 35-m (115-ft) schooner *Amphitrite*, built by Camper and

On 25 May 1893 a crowd gathered on the *banks of the Thames* to watch the *first race* of the royal yacht Britannia.

was fast in wind, but not so good in light airs. In spite of its tonnage it was steered with a long tiller. Dunraven's challenge never took place because the New York Yacht Club and the Royal Yacht Squadron could not reach agreement on the conditions for the meeting or how to measure the handicap of the contestants.

How could two yachts with different characteristics compete with each other on an equal footing? Or, to put it another way, how could a fair handicap be calculated to equalise the chances of a sailing boat that was slower from the beginning? It was necessary to find a way of bringing tonnages and complex ratios into play to solve this awkward problem. In the summer of 1855 the Thames Register was created, followed by several other means of calculation, none of which was really satisfactory. Then in 1880 Dixon Kemp, a British specialist, suggested a new method. Born on the Isle of Wight in 1839 and a writer for *Field*, he was a man of few words except in his writing. He dressed more like an ordinary man than a yachtsman, and thought there were only two people in Great Britain who could write validly about sailing there, and that he was one of them. In 1870 and 1871 he had accompanied Ashbury to New York at the time of his challenge, in 1875 he was involved in the formation of the Yacht Racing Association, and the following year he published a reference book *Yacht Designing*. The formula he advocated led to the production of narrow yachts heavily weighted with ballast, real floating corridors.

On 25 May 1893, a crowd gathered on the banks of the Thames to watch the first race of the royal yacht *Britannia*. George Watson had spent all of the previous Christmas designing the plans for two yachts, practically sister ships. The first for the Prince of Wales, Victoria's oldest son and the future King of England, was named *Britannia*, the second, commanded by Lord Dunraven was the *Valkyrie II*. It was a superb race. The yachts were 35 m (115 ft) in length and carried 930 m^2 (10,010 ft^2) of sail. At the same time, a Scottish syndicate had placed an order with the young Fife for his first large yacht, *Santanita*. The same year, Phelps Caroll, an American, had asked the architect, Nat Herreshoff to design the *Navahoe*, a 38-m (125-ft) yacht with 1,000 m^2 (10,763 ft^2) of sail, and brought it to Great Britain to face the British yachts. The Royal Thames Yacht Club had hired a special train from London to Gravesend to watch *Britannia* sail. However, when they saw the new yacht, the experts, or those who thought of themselves as experts, shook their heads. They were shocked by the Royal yacht's bow. Spoon-shaped, she had dispensed with the traditional bowsprit. A torrent of slanderous comments was heard, 'Gratuitously stupid, hideous'. At the downwind mark, *Irex*

Nicholson for Colonel MacGregor, which won 15 out of 25 races in her class. There was also rivalry between the designers. In 1890 alone, 60 yachts were under construction in Great Britain, 22 to Fife's design, 19 to Watson's and 11 to Payne's.

Minerva, built to Fife's design and 12.2 m (40 ft) long at the waterline, was overwhelmingly superior to the opposing American boats until she came up against the *Gossoon* in the races at Boston's Eastern Yacht Club. This lifting-keel yacht, 11.98 m (38 ft) at the waterline, was lightly built of wood on a steel frame, and was sailed against the *Minerva* with skill and enthusiasm by the Adams brothers, two young yachtsmen, demonstrating the strength of the design of the American architect William Burgess. Had the time come for the English to accept defeat? Lord Dunraven was the owner of a large estate in Ireland and a strong personality. This aristocrat had been a war reporter, and had hunted enthusiastically with Buffalo Bill in Nebraska. He was a good violinist and had dreamt of being a musician. He was also a gifted writer. At the age of 46, on board John Jameson's schooner the *Goelette* he discovered sailing, and went on to become an expert. The author of a very lucid treatise on navigation, he demonstrated a long-term vision. But his quick temper and anger spoiled his good qualities, and this charming and intelligent man lacked both moderation and judgement.

In 1889 he built the 26 m (85 ft) *Valkyrie*, to Watson's design. In its first season the yacht carried off 23 cups from 33 races. The boat

which dated from 1887, was only 46 seconds behind the new sailing ships which, close hauled on the following tack demonstrated their superiority and silenced all the critics. Another very soberly written criticism highlighting the thoughtlessness in *Britannia's* lay-out appeared in the magazine *Le Yacht*: 'it is up to the yachtsman to decide whether racing ought to return to being a pleasing sport or a bitter struggle in fistfuls of pounds sterling in machine-yachts, uncomfortable if not uninhabitable, and built to last for only a few months'. Everything is relative, a piano was included in *Britannia's* fixtures, even if it was an upright piano. And *Britannia* lasted longer than a few months. In the course of her career she took part in 630 races, winning 365 of them. On the death of King George, as stipulated by her owner, she was scuttled at sea.

The confrontation between *Britannia* and *Valkyrie II* went in favour of Lord Dunraven's yacht with 11 wins against the Prince of Wales's eight. So *Valkyrie II* set off confidently for the United States to meet her adversary from the New York Yacht Club. Facing her, the American *Vigilant* had an even larger sail area, and needed 70 strapping men to control her. Lord Dunraven, beaten, issued a new challenge with *Valkyrie III* but the remarkable work of Watson, the boatyard, the craftsmen and the sailors who managed to produce and handle an exceptional boat was marred by his bad-tempered outbursts. The race in England between *Britannia* and *Navahoe* was a superb confrontation with the two yachts running side by side, with never more than 150 m (490 ft)

between them. The British cutter won by a narrow margin, but lost after a protest brought by her opponent. In her first season *Britannia* won 20 out of the 38 races she competed in. The following year an incident occurred in a race at Holy Loch. *Satanita*, a 38 m (124 ft) cutter designed by J. M. Soper for A. B. Clarke, was the first to cross the line on a stretch of water littered with spectator boats. *Satanita*, very fast in the fresh breeze, was a formidable adversary. When she was going at full speed, a small yacht suddenly appeared under her bow. *Satanita* luffed to avoid her, tipped over, rammed *Valkyrie II* with the top of the mast and split her open to the waterline. Dunraven's yacht drifted first on to the motor yacht *Thebe*, mortally wounding a member of her crew, then on to the *Vanduara*, another motor yacht, and finally sank. Sir Maurice Fitzgerald, an owner of racing yachts bought the re-floated *Valkyrie II* in 1897. The races took place on narrow tracts of water, further cluttered by yachts at anchor so that the crowds of admirers could watch the racing. The danger to the sailing boats, some of which were almost 40 m (131 ft) in length, was enormous. A less tragic incident happened during a race from Dover to Boulogne.

In a good north-easterly wind, *Vendetta* crossed the line first, but collided with *Valkyrie II* who lost her top mast. Then *Britannia* collided with *Valkyrie II*, tore off her rigging and smashed *Vendetta's* bowsprit. *Britannia's* mainsail ripped on *Vendetta's* cross-trees. There was total confusion, and the crew of *Valkyrie II* had to saw off *Britannia's* bowsprit to free themselves! After the cavalcade of *Valkyrie's* and the

ABOVE
In 1893, Valkyrie II, built to George Watson's design, met the American defender Vigilant *in the United States, but failed to beat her.*

FACING PAGE, TOP
George V, the owner of the exceptional royal yacht Britannia, *is one of the great figures from the Edwardian age of yachting.*

FACING PAGE, BOTTOM
Because of his changing moods, Lord Dunraven spoilt the very real chances of his superb yacht the Valkyrie III.

FOLLOWING DOUBLE PAGE
Dora Hugo and the wife of the painter, *painting by Paul César Helleu (1859–1927).*

Lipton, a wealthy grocer, shunned by the British gentry yet given a title by the Queen, tried to win back the America's Cup on five occasions.

deterioration in the relationship between the United States and Great Britain caused by Lord Dunraven's outbursts, it fell to a commoner, one of those upstarts who would never gain admittance to the Royal Yacht Squadron, to restore Britain's honour.

The Liptons had been chased out of Ireland by the famines and had settled in Glasgow. The father of the family found employment as a worker in a paper factory and in 1850, the Liptons used their savings to set up a small grocery shop. Thomas, the last of their three children was born on 10 May of the same year. The youngest of the family, he went to the local school and learnt to read and write, but he loved commerce and from the age of 6 or 7, he helped his parents in their little shop. The business didn't prosper and so Thomas left school when he was 10 to earn his own keep. An errand boy, he loved the sea and dreamt of boats, and got taken on as a ship's boy between Glasgow and Belfast. When he was 15 he

invested his savings in a deck-class ticket to New York. He found work on a tobacco plantation in Virginia, then in a rice-processing factory in Carolina, and finally on the grocery counter of a large New York department store. There he came across publicity and American sales methods; he also learnt good manners and was promoted. When he returned to Scotland aged 18, he had $500 of savings. He treated himself to the luxury of arriving at his parents' home in a cab, thereby exciting the entire neighbourhood.

Thomas Lipton opened his own grocery shop when he was 21. He used the publicity methods he had learnt in the United States, keeping his prices low by buying his produce direct from Ireland was a success from the start. Less than ten years later he was the owner of some 20 shops, had become a millionaire and had given his mother a barouche. He was 40 when his parents died but he had already started another venture. He wanted to make tea a popular drink that everyone could afford. Coffee trees in Ceylon were being attacked by an infection and the plantations were in a state of collapse. Lipton bought seven holdings at a low price, and set 3,000 men to work on the 1,500 ha (3706.5 acres) pulling out the coffee trees. He lived an austere, celibate life, building his success through work. He was intelligent, gifted with a remarkable ability to adapt, and had all the charm of a brilliant, well-mannered man. He always dressed elegantly, wearing a white spotted bow tie in both winter and summer. He was a multimillionaire but was not accepted in society. However, in 1895, he became a rotak warrant holder 'By Appointment' to the Queen. He met Lord and Lady Breadalbane on a train. Lord Breadalbane was a Knight of the Garter, an eminent member of the Liberal Party, and the owner of a vast estate. These nobles became the wealthy grocer's best friends and he invited them to stay at his chateau at Osidge, and to visit him in Ceylon.

A fund had been started for the Queen's jubilee, but £125,000 was needed to pay for a meal for the poor. Lipton signed a cheque for this sum, asking to remain anonymous, but there was speculation in the press and among the gentry over the identity of the generous donor. A skilfully planned indiscretion eventually revealed Lipton's name enabling him to benefit from some amazing publicity. A total of 400,000 people were brought together for the meal and Lipton accompanied the Prince of Wales on a visit to the 'Dinner for the Poor'. The Princess of Wales started the Alexandra Foundation and Lipton signed a cheque for $500,000. Thomas Lipton's fame crossed the Atlantic and he was welcomed by a horde of reporters when he arrived in New York. All this fuss was excellent for business, even in the United States, and on 18 January 1898 he was received by Queen Victoria at Osborne House and given a title. *Vanity Fair* said appreciatively: 'this title rewards both an excellent man and an excellent business'. But even though he was now Sir Thomas, Lipton he was still only a wealthy grocer to some members of the nobility. However, he was a good friend of the Prince of Wales. Queen Victoria's son had become the arbitrator of European society and each year he followed the same unchanging pattern, visiting Balmoral in Scotland in the autumn for shooting, London for the winter, Paris and Biarritz in the spring, a cruise in the Mediterranean, Epsom and Ascot in June for the races, visiting the country in July, and Cowes for the month of August. Edward, who had been made commodore of the Squadron in 1882, would strut about on the lawn in a white cap, with a Havana cigar in his mouth, an ebony cane in his hand, accompanied by one of his lady friends of the moment, Alice Keppel or the actress, Lily Langtree or sometimes by his wife, the Princess Alexandra. When he was sailing on *Britannia*, Victoria would train her opera glasses on the yacht to see which one of his mistresses he had taken on board that day.

Undoubtedly it was the Prince of Wales who suggested that Lipton should challenge for the America's Cup. The millionaire hadn't

shown any interest in yachting before 1888. However, he realised that trying to win the trophy would reward him on two fronts. Despite his recent elevation to the peerage, his fortune and a prince's friendship, the majority of the English nobility refused to acknowledge him and fitting out a large yacht and taking it to the United States ought to open some hitherto closed doors for her owner. The other was a commercial advantage. A challenge would provide Lipton and his products with some profitable publicity in the American market. Lipton's ventures had never run into difficulty so following on from Dunraven's tantrums, this immigrant's son would not be averse to re-establishing the United Kingdom's reputation and to succeed where the nobles who snubbed him had failed.

Joseph Chamberlain, the Minister for Colonial Affairs, was anxious that Dunraven's blunders should not to be repeated and asked Lipton to save the Anglo-American relationship. Sir Thomas bought a 85 m (278 ft) steam-driven yacht, fitted out with all the comforts of a luxury home, and gave it a new name *Erin*. He issued his challenge in the name of the Royal Ulster Yacht Club on 6 August 1898, as the Royal Yacht Squadron had not deigned to admit him as a member. Lipton ordered the *Shamrock* from William Fife junior. She was a very light cutter, 27.27 m (89 ft) long at the waterline, carried 1,200 m² (12,916 ft²) of sail and was sailed by a crew of 40 men. The yacht was launched on 24 June 1899 and then towed across the Atlantic by *Erin*. Thomas Lipton had all the qualities needed to please the Americans. He was a charming, self-made man who combined financial success with generosity. When *Shamrock* met *Columbia* in 1899, Lipton followed the races from on board his steamer *Erin* and invited 90 guests for lunch on the deck. Theodore Roosevelt came, as did Mark Twain, Thomas Edison and New York's most elegant ladies. *Columbia* had been built by 'the Sorcerer of Bristol,' Nathaniel Herreschoff. Having lost the three races of his first challenge, Thomas Lipton, a good sport admitted: 'Such a trophy cannot be won at the first attempt,' and he returned in 1901 with *Shamrock II*, designed by Watson. Watson's design was faster than her opponent's in the first race. *Shamrock II* rounded the windward mark in the lead, but on the long return Charlie Barr's cunning and tactical sense managed to catch up with the British yacht and crossed the line 35 seconds in front. In the second race, *Shamrock II*'s helm, Scudamore, had the best start on the triangular course and *Columbia* only managed to nibble away at a tiny part of her lead. It was only on the last leg that the American yacht managed to get in the lead by tacking and won. In the third race it seemed that all the British hopes were justified. Charlie Barr had the best start, with Scudamore three seconds behind him. But on the first leg, the British yacht took the lead and was 49 seconds in the lead at the buoy. On the last leg Charlie Barr, using every ounce of concentration, caught up inch by inch, and the two yachts crossed the finishing line together. After a 30-mile course *Columbia* won on handicap by 41 seconds.

Much encouraged, Lipton declared 'I will return'. To face *Shamrock III* in 1903, the 'Bristol Sorcerer' dared to design a yacht of disproportionate size. Financed by a syndicate headed by William Rockfeller and Cornelius Vanderbilt, *Reliance* was 27.40 m (90 ft) on the waterline, had 43.6 m (143 ft) of deck and

measured 61 m (196.5 ft) from the tip of her bowsprit to the end of her 43 m (141 ft) boom. Her spinnaker boom was 25 m (82 ft) long, the mainsail 4 tonne (8,818 lb) in weight and 64 men were needed to handle the 1,486 m² (15,995 ft²) of sail. *Shamrock III* being the same length on the waterline, but more modest in her other dimensions, was slightly faster on the beat in the first race. Charles Barr craftily avoided keeping too close to the wind, making up in speed what he was losing in direction and reached the buoy three minutes in the lead. On the downwind leg, *Reliance*, with her flatter shape, took off and won by more than seven minutes. The second race confirmed her superiority, and then in the third race, with a light wind *Reliance* had a significant lead when the fog came in and Wringe, the English skipper, lost his way.

In 1898 Lipton decided to enjoy life so went public, issuing shares in his company while keeping the majority interest for himself. He discovered worldly pleasures and receptions and was often accompanied by the Prince of Wales who snubbed protocol by increasing his amorous adventures, provoking scandals both large and small. In 1901, the newly crowned King Edward VII narrowly escaped serious injury on board *Shamrock II* when the mast fell on to the deck.

Lipton went cruising in the Mediterranean aboard *Erin II*, and received the cream of European society on board in Monaco, Greece and Italy. He made five attempts to bring the America's Cup back to England. In 1920 *Shamrock II* came very close to winning and in 1930, even though he was 80, Lipton had a final attempt. A good loser, his persistence had made him immensely popular on both sides of the Atlantic, but it wasn't until the end of his life that the Royal Yacht Squadron finally accepted into their ranks the man who had done so much for the honour of British yachting.

At the same time a new generation of steam-driven yachts was being developed whose owners looked condescendingly at the sailing yachts, for steam-driven yachts furnished their owners and their guests with the greatest refinement. One of them, Cecil Leigh's *White Heather*, which was often anchored in the Solent, was famous for the luxury of life on board. Every morning boats went out to her carrying boxes of strawberries and cartons of cream for the afternoon receptions. *Cassandra*, which measured nearly 100 m (328 ft), had a uniformed crew of 64, including seven officers and masters, a head chef and his assistant and nine stewards. Lord Belfast, one of the members of the Royal Yacht Squadron had a particularly fast yacht, the *Waterwitch*, and he used to enjoy showing his heels to the Royal Navy by overtaking their ships, until the day the Navy bought *Waterwitch* so they could copy her lines.

Having lost the three races of his first challenge, Thomas Lipton, a good sport admitted, 'Such a trophy can not be won at the first attempt'.

At the end of the nineteenth century, the British fleet was estimated to have 6,000 steam-powered and sailing yachts. It gave employment to 35,000 people: workers in the shipyards, crews, sail-makers, riggers, and fitters. Those in the highest echelons of the aristocracy sailed, the Prince of Wales on his 216-ton cutter, *Aline*, the Marquis of Anglesey on the 311-ton *Santa Cecilia*, the Duke of Hamilton had bought *Thistle*, and the Duke of Bedford, the Duke of St Albans and the Prince of Battenburg would all have been ashamed not to own their own yachts. Even some ladies, although they weren't admitted into the masculine intimacy of the yacht clubs ventured to take the helm, competing in ladies races despite the constraints of long dresses, hats and occasionally parasols.

In 1901 the Duchess of Bedford hired the 74-m (243-ft) *Sapphine*, for a cruise to Salzburg, bought the yacht in 1903 and brought it back it to the Orkneys. A short while before her death in 1901, Queen Victoria ordered a new yacht. The *Victoria and Albert III*, 116 m (380 ft) long, was so heavily equipped with fixtures and fittings that when it was launched it had a 24° list, and needed two years' work to make it seaworthy.

In the years before the First World War, some superb yachts came out of the shipyards of the Clyde and the Solent. Nicholson's square-rigged cutter, was made for Renée Calame, an independently wealthy inhabitant of Nantes. *Orion*, a 44-m (144-ft) square-rigged schooner, which was first named *Sylvana*, was built for Colonel Morgan by Camper and Nicholson. *Tuiga's* 15 m (50 ft) of international tonnage was a design commissioned from Fife by the Duke of Mediancelli, a friend of the King of Spain. It was also William Fife junior who designed *Moonbeam II*, a 42-ton cutter launched in 1899, and *Moonbeam III*, a square-rigged cutter whose overall length was 30.6 m (100 ft), and whose deck measured 2.4 m (80 ft). She was built at Fairlie using

mahogany planking on an oak frame, for the London lawyer, Charles Plumtree Johnson, the son of Queen Victoria's doctor and a member of the Royal Yacht Squadron and the Royal Thames Yacht Club. The third generation member of the Fife dynasty was undoubtedly the most gifted. He also designed two elegant cutters, *Nan*, 13.5 m (44 ft) long at the waterline and built by the Irishman Thomas Burrows in 1896, and two years later *Yum* 10.04 m (33 ft) long at the waterline built by Mr Cummins, also from Ireland.

In 1906, the British yachting fleet had double the tonnage of the rest of Europe, however, the period ended with a certain loss of affection for these giant, ruinously expensive yachts, and spectators no longer flocked to the banks of the Thames and the Solent. Many yachtsmen preferred to sail on more moderately sized yachts, which needed fewer crew members. A 1903 trial monotype, the South Coast One Design, at 22 m (72 ft) overall didn't achieve the success expected of it. Even the extremely rich Lipton asked for smaller boats to be used for the America's Cup races. He suggested using yachts of 33 m (108 ft) in overall length, 23 m (75 ft) on the waterline. The New York Yacht Club declined with the comment 'Such sailing boats would be of insignificant size and power'.
War broke out and for a whole class of those privileged by birth and fortune, the luxuries and easy life of the Edwardian era quickly belonged to a bygone age. And since *America's* victory in 1851, it had had to be admitted that wealth, boldness and innovation were to be found on the other side of the ocean.

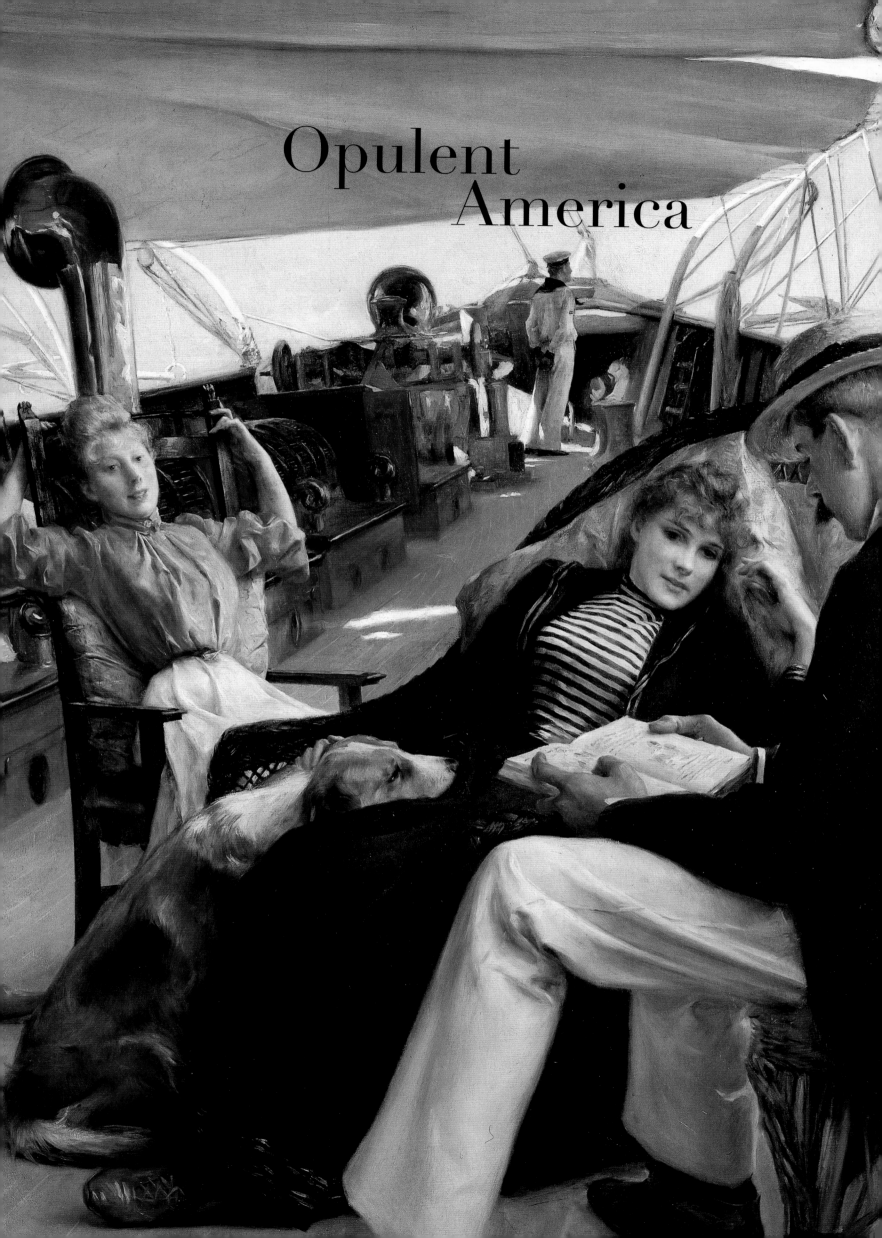

Opulent
America

In Great Britain yachting was a way of life. In the new America it was a sign of power and success. The Stevens family provides a good example of the fortunes of the conquerors of the New World. An English lawyer's clerk landed in America in 1669. His son, a tradesman and ship owner acquired vast areas of land in New Jersey. Then in 1749, one of the third generation, John Stevens, served as a captain under Washington, reached the rank of colonel, became treasurer of the State of New Jersey, and added to the family's land-holdings

On 30 July 1844, nine yachtsmen met together on board the schooner Gimcrack
to form the New York Yacht Club with John Stevens as its first commodore.

where a century and a half later the Stevens Institute of Technology would be founded. The Stevens were gifted engineers and John designed and tested the first propellers for steamboats. His son Edwin was involved in the first railway projects and Robert Livingstone, another of his sons, became a master of naval architecture, designing steamers and ferries and inventing the T rail. In 1836 he designed a very fast, ballasted 33.55-m (110-ft) sailing sloop, the *Maria* for his own use. His brother John Cox Stevens, a lover of cricket and boats, owned the 15-m (50-ft) schooner *Gimcrack*. On the evening of 30 July 1844 he invited nine yachtsmen to meet on board. They were drinking and joking in one of those wardroom conversations that constitute one of the delights of sailing. Eight of them owned yachts, and in the course of the conversation they decided to set up a yacht club to be called the New York Yacht Club and chose John Stevens to be its commodore. The New

Yorkers in those days used to picnic on a level section of the riverbank that they called the Champs-Elysées. Commodore Stevens had a Gothic-style cottage there, which became the association's first clubhouse. Convinced of the supremacy of American yachts and with the boldness of those who have conquered all, seven members of the club, under the guidance of John Stevens, formed a syndicate to challenge British yachts. They ordered the design of a schooner from a 31-year-old architect, George Steer, called it *America*, crossed the Atlantic and on 22 August 1851, won the race round the Isle of Wight and carried the first prize, the 100-Guinea Cup, off to the United States. The most famous page in the history of yachting had just been written.

American yachting in the Edwardian era was centred round two groups. The first, the millionaires who provided dynamism and success and the second, although they were

probably much the same, those devotees of the sport who would defend the trophy taken at Cowes and take a major stake in American sailing through the demonstration of the skill of her architects, of the power of the financiers and of the dexterity of her skippers and their crews.

For businessmen, industrialists and

bankers, owning a yacht became a duty. 'I have bought a large telescope,' stated one financier, 'and as soon as I opened it I knew that I would like to own a yacht'. Wall Street was creating millionaires at a rate unheard of, and there was no leisure activity more luxurious or desirable for these *nouveaux riches* than the possession of a large yacht. As J. D. Kelley commented in 1890, about yachting and money. 'You must have a lot of it, and it isn't enough to spend it grudgingly. Your fortune will run through your hands like water'.

Henry Clay Pierce an oil magnate asked the banker John Pierpont Morgan 'How much does it cost to run a yacht? You can't afford it? Why not? If you ask that sort of question you haven't the means to own a yacht'.

Even if this dialogue is of doubtful authenticity, it bears witness to the spirit of these multimillionaires who worked unrelentingly to make their fortunes often with a complete absence of scruple in the face of financial risks. They loved to flaunt their wealth and disparage the British gentry, 'that caste of well-behaved idlers rich in experience who had time to sail all the year round but had treasures shallower than a well and lighter than a church door'. They didn't have the time to indulge in such luxuries: *time is money!* They preferred the certainty of mechanical propulsion to the hazards of sailing. The banker Edward S. Jaffrey said, 'We are all businessmen. We have neither the time nor the inclination to stay becalmed for days on an oily sea. With steamers yachtsmen can go where and when they want'. He added, 'I have observed the picturesque character and weaknesses of yachts with sails'. He owned a 52-m (170-ft) steam-driven yacht and lived in a waterfront property during the summer, travelling to Manhattan every morning on his boat, the *Stranger*. William Astor, another owner of great wealth of that time, used to start his day with a dip in the sea, then he would swim to his 67-m (220-ft) yacht

Nourmahal, have a shower, get dressed for the day, eat his breakfast and, by the time he had finished, his boat was nearing the landing stage and his Manhattan offices. 'As William P. Stephens said, An American capitalist's life both through choice and necessity is so closely linked to his business affairs that he can't imagine moments of pleasure and relaxation unless they are connected to the notion of speed'. Certainly cost couldn't come into it, including the crew, coal and maintenance the *Nourmahal* cost her owner $75,000 (at today's value) to run each year. John A. Morris's *Cora* employed 12 professionals on a $100,000 budget. The living quarters comprised a dining room, boudoir, small and large saloons, guest cabins and the owner's suite of rooms. Its estimated value today would be $3 million,

It was a contest among Yankee businessmen, the sharks of the financial world speculating on Wall Street, becoming wealthy through mining, railways, transport or banking, to see who owned the longest, the most luxurious and the fastest yacht.

but this investment wasn't just a way to waste money. The yachts were also used for entertaining, business meetings, and for their owner's public relations.

The competition that these sharks of the financial world engaged in, started on Wall Street and extended to their boats: i.e. who owned the longest, the most luxurious and fastest yacht. Jay Gould was one example of this race of Yankee businessmen. His critics said he had built his fortune by speculations verging on the fraudulent. When he merged his Kansas Pacific Railroad with Union Pacific he received a $3 million bonus that remained hidden from his shareholders. He grew 8,000 orchids on his 500 ha (1,235 acre) property and the swimming pool was so big that the swimming teacher used to use a boat. In 1883 he had the yacht *Atlanta* built. She was 70 m (230 ft) long, cost $250,000 at the time, employed a crew of 52 and was ostentatiously luxurious. Her dining room could accommodate 32 people and was furnished with superb tapestries, electric lights, and a machine capable of producing half a tonne (1,102 lb) of ice a day. Even so, the New York Yacht Club and the Eastern Yacht Club rejected his membership application. That wasn't a problem! Gould set up his own club, the American Yacht Club, which, he proudly stated, gathered together the strongest concentration of capital for this type of association. Based in the well sheltered anchorage of Bay Ridge, to the west of New York, the American Yacht Club soon earned another reputation for the excellent cuisine enjoyed on her admirably shady terraces, for its pleasant atmosphere and for pretty women. Its situation was an ideal starting point for East

River and Long Island Sound whose small deep bays and little islands were a paradise for sailing enthusiasts. However, it wasn't the only significant club in the area. Larchmont Yacht Club, based in a splendid property on the coast had a breathtaking view of Long Island Sound. Howard Gould's *Niagra* was a 74-m (243-ft), rigged three-masted steamer whose 11-m (36-ft) long saloon was in the style of the Renaissance and whose annual running costs were as much as $125,000 in those days. Cornelius Vanderbilt had started to accumulate wealth when he was 16 by borrowing $100 from his mother. Vanderbilt who was frivolous, self-centred, and merciless towards his competitors, built a shipping company that half

In 1907 an elegant crowd invaded Larchmont Yacht Club's terraces when 110 yachts were racing in Long Island Sound.

a century later was 66 boats strong. In 1853, by which time he had become the richest man in America, he decided to enjoy life. He ordered the first American steam-driven yacht, an 82-m (269-ft) paddleboat the *North Star*. It was a floating palace with 10 cabins, armchairs and sofas made of rosewood, a dining room, a banqueting hall with a marble floor decorated with medallions of Christopher Columbus, George Washington and other heroes from American history. He engaged a former clipper captain, Asa Aldridge, took his wife Sophie on board, along with their 12 children, a doctor and a chaplain... *North Star* crossed the Atlantic, burning 42 tonnes (92,594 lb) of coal a day. On arrival in England, Vanderbilt invited 400 personages for a tour round the Isle of Wight, but in spite of his invitations not a single crowned head or member of the royal family came aboard. A journalist ventured to remark however that, 'from now on it is time for the term of upstart to be honoured'. Cornelius Vanderbilt was finally achieved his ambition at Kronstadt when the Grand Duke Constantin visited his yacht and Vanderbilt's example led Tsar Alexander to order a steam-driven yacht. After this cruise in European waters, Cornelius sold *North Star* and gave up sailing. On his death in 1877 his fortune was estimated at $100 million. Following family

tradition, William Kinan Vanderbilt had the *Alva* built. She was a three-master furnished with two boilers and was the longest and most costly yacht of her time. Having sailed to the West Indies and Europe, the boat sank after running aground. William K. Vanderbilt immediately ordered a new, larger boat, the 88-m (289-ft) *Valiant* with 20 cabins, manned by a crew of 62 and which crossed the Atlantic in seven days. The multimillionaire had spent more than a million dollars on the construction and fitting out of his yacht. Parisian decorators had been called in to furnish the main saloon in the style of Louis XIV, and he boasted that his boat was longer than Queen Victoria's.

His nephew, Cornelius Vanderbilt III owned the second *North Star*, which was crammed with works of art. His wife Grace, who owned the grandiose property of Beaulieu at Newport, went to Cowes every summer on this tall, long-hulled yacht to see the royal family and more particularly, to be seen by them and thereby earned her nickname 'The Kingfisher'.

One colourful figure of the extremely rich of America was James Gordon Bennett, the son of the founder of the *New York Herald*. His father, a Scottish immigrant who had

Vanderbilt, frivolous, self-centred, and merciless towards his competitors, had started to accumulate wealth when he was 16 by borrowing $100 from his mother. On his death his fortune was estimated at $100 million.

created this gleefully scandalous daily paper, was treated as an outcast by Good Society. His son very quickly gained the reputation of a flamboyant libertine, creating scandals purely for the fun of it. For his sixteenth birthday his father gave him the *Rebecca*, a sloop measuring 21 m (70 ft) on the waterline. Four years later he owned the 32-m (105-ft) *Henrietta*. When James Gordon Bennett became the sole owner of the *New York Herald* he earned $30 million a year and spent them just as quickly on his dissipated lifestyle. After his engagement was broken off in 1877 he moved to Paris, started a European edition of his paper and sailed his steamboat *Namounia* across the Atlantic, the Mediterranean and the Aegean Sea, entertaining in her 36-m² (387.5-ft²) saloon. This 70-m (230-ft) yacht, which was capable of speeds up to 14 knots, had maple, walnut and teak panelling and the floors were covered with oriental carpets. This steamer cost her owner $48,000 a year to run including maintenance and the salaries of a crew of 50. The *Lysistrata*, ordered in Scotland and launched in 1901 was almost 100 m (328 ft) in length and cost the fabulous sum of $18 million. Bennett took his numerous mistresses aboard. The fittings included a Turkish bath and a stable complete with two cows and an electric milking machine for a supply of fresh milk every morning.

James Gordon Bennett was a tyrannical boss who had a horror of card games. He used to go through the guest's and sailor's luggage and if he found a pack of cards he would tear up the aces then replace the pack where he had found it. He also had a phobia of beards. It was said of him that, 'When sober he had the worst defects of the Scots and when drunk those of the Irish'.

Once he welcomed a theatre troop on board and being pleased by their performance he ordered the boat to cast off and stay at sea until the troop had performed their entire repertoire. When one of the cows in the stable died, James Gordon Bennett went in search of another one of the same breed to replace her. He had taken one of his journalists with him and when the cow had been bought, Bennett returned in his car leaving the journalist to walk back with the animal. The owner of the *New York Herald* died in 1918 at 77 years of age held in contempt and dread, and practically ruined.

The banker John Pierpont Morgan was another of these fabulously rich yachtsmen. He was 1.8 m (6 ft) tall and had an impressively powerful build. His eyes were piercing under their thick brows and he had a bushy moustache below his strong, rounded nose.

ABOVE
North Star *the first American steam yacht was built in 1853 for Cornelius Vanderbilt, the richest man in America.*

FOLLOWING DOUBLE PAGE
William K. Vanderbilt, on the left in a deckchair, sailing in the Mediterranean on board Alva in 1887–1888. In the centre are two of his children Willie and Consuela, she would later become the Duchess of Alva. In the hammock is his wife Alva, who after her divorce went on to marry Olivier Belmont, seated to the left on a carpet.

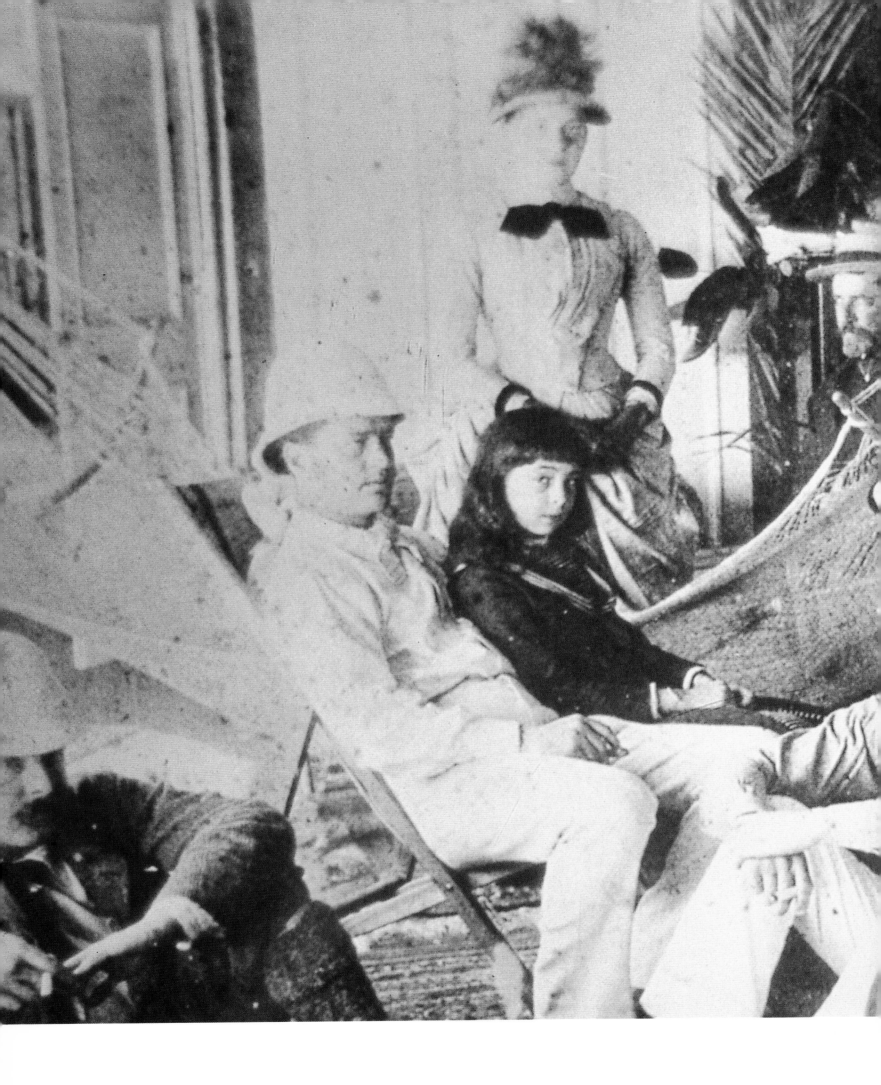

Cornelius Vanderbilt used to go sailing on North Star,
which had rosewood armchairs and a dining room paved with marble.
His son William Kinan continued the family tradition by having the Alva
built, **the longest, most costly yacht of her time.**

The financier liked to spend the whole summer on board his yacht *Corsair*, moored at a Manhattan quay near his offices. He entertained and held meetings there in the privacy and intimacy of his stateroom. He said 'one can do business with anyone but one must only be surrounded by gentlemen when boating'. In 1895 Morgan paid $45 million to Manhattan for some land and gave it to the New York Yacht Club so that a clubhouse could be built on it. *Corsair II*, 62 m (203 ft) on the waterline and built in 1892, was requisitioned six years later during the Spanish–American war. Renamed the *USS Gloucester* she covered herself in glory by sinking one Spanish torpedo boat and capturing another. In 1899 Morgan ordered the 92-m (302-ft) *Corsair III*, which was capable of speeds up to 19 knots and which would stay in the family's possession for more than 30 years. One of his associates, Anthony J. Drexel had asked Watson to design the *Margarita* for him. She stood out not only through her double hull and ten watertight bulkheads but also by the sophistication of her fittings. She had steam heating, air conditioning 800 electric light bulbs, a machine capable of producing over half a tonne (1,200 lb) of ice per day, and Chippendale furniture. This 100-m (328-ft) long ship run by 93 staff was later sold to the Marquis of Anglesey who gave it to the Navy to use during the First World War. These symbols of success weren't

always associated with a mature age. When he was a student, George Lander, heir to a steel king, owned the 42-m (138-ft) schooner *Endymion* employing 20 sailors. In 1885 John Jay Phelps invited his friends on board the 35-m (115 ft) *Brunhilde* to celebrate the end of his studies and they set out together on a world tour lasting three years.

Often the yacht owners were colourful characters. It was certainly true of John Aspinall, William's son, and president of the Pacific Mail Steamship Company. John was a preacher in the Episcopal Church but also passionate about steam-driven machinery. He was a sailor, engineer, and naval architect and would go on to own about 12 yachts. The New York lawyer Elbridge T. Gerry was one of the first to have a generator installed in his yacht aptly named *Electra*. A journalist, invited on board for a cruise, was alone in the dining room at breakfast time, and was offered oysters, Westphalian ham, roast turkey, fillet of beef, pastries, ice creams and Californian grapes, all washed down with Bordeaux wine.

Alongside these multimillionaires who were keen to appear real mariners, were those like William Henn who were the genuine article. This Irishman, who had served in the Royal Navy and had then emigrated to the United States, shared his love of sailing with

his wife and their pets. On board the *Galatea* were greyhounds, a racoon and a monkey named Peggy who joined in the manoeuvres wearing a sailor suit embroidered with her name. On her husband's death in 1887 Mrs Henn carried on sailing, covering some 50,000 miles.

Although 200 large steam ships were sailing under the flag of the New York Yacht Club in 1900, sailing was the domain of the true amateurs. They hadn't waited for the defence of the America's Cup to get hold of sloops, cutters and schooners that took part in lively competitions. Sandbaggers were over-canvassed dinghies balanced by some 30 sacks of sand that the crews had to move on each tack. Betting brought an additional spice to the contests and sometimes the stakes for a single day's racing were as high as $50,000. It was the done thing to take part on these occasions, even though it was not customary to race on a Sunday. Wall Street brokers came to the banks to take part in social events that didn't hinder business relationships. The most aggressive crews possible manned the sandbaggers. It wasn't unusual for a crew that had been beaten on the water to look for their opponents on dry land to continue the fight. If there was a protest the jury was wise to find a safe place before giving its verdict. William

T. Garner, the vice commodore of the New York Yacht Club, had the *Mowhawk* built in 1875. She was a schooner with a lifting keel, measured 36 m (118 ft) at the waterline, with a 9-m (29.5 ft) beam and drew 1.8 m (6 ft). On 20 July 1876 a sudden squall capsized the yacht: the tonnes of moveable ballast and furniture slipped, injuring the owner and his wife and killing two guests. However, this accident didn't deter the enthusiasts. As W. Stephens, the columnist, commented, 'some are only motivated by a typically American grand principle namely to own the world's greatest object'.

An annual ritual brought American

yachts together. Races were held until the end of June and then the yachts of the New York Yacht Club, sometimes as many as 200 of them, gathered in Glen Cove Bay to the west of Long Island, under the commodore's orders, for a group cruise. An amazing hierarchy was set up comprising, commodore, vice commodore, captains, lieutenants, ensigns and subalterns. They sailed in a squadron and anchored in the many natural harbours along the coast. While the male owners would dive in for a morning swim at dawn, an unwritten law forbade the ladies to come on deck before the hoisting of the colours

ABOVE
Margarita's saloon was decorated in the style of Louis XV. With her carpets, sofas and massive desk, this yacht was one of the most lavish of her time.

ABOVE
In 1886, three American schooners, Henrietta, Fleetwing *and* Vesta *raced across the Atlantic in the middle of winter. Each owner had pledged a $30,000 stake.*

RIGHT
Yachtswomen around 1892.

While the male owners would dive in for a morning swim at dawn, an unwritten *law forbade the ladies to come on deck before the hoisting of the colours at 8 a.m.*

at 8 o'clock. In the evenings, the yachts were lit with a multitude of lanterns. People were invited on board one another's yachts and the harbours were busy with the constant coming and going of dinghies. These cruises were the setting for parties, entertainments, fireworks and balls in 'mansions', those huge residences at Newport or on the coast. It was in Newport Bay too that the Goelet Cup was held. Its patron Ogden Goelet, financed the prize of $15,000 for sloops, and $30,000 for schooners. The Venetian parade formed a long luminous snake across the harbour. The cruise took the yachts to Martha's Vineyard, the island where Bostonians had their summer homes and the conviviality between yachtsmen from the same or supposedly the same worlds wasn't hindered by ideas of propriety. As James Gilroy recalled, 'life on the large American yachts is more lively than on British yachts. First of all the yachts have to moor by New York town with all its possible distractions. Secondly, some of the owners enjoy their newly acquired wealth in a vigorous manner'. Not everything was in the best of taste...

One yacht was famous for frequent belly dancing on its aft deck, another for its owner's 'press button' cabin. One button controlled the music, another unveiled the bar and a third one opened a bulkhead to reveal the intimate moments of guests who had already retired.

Sherman Hoyt tells how one day at Newport the calm of a Sunday morning was broken by a noisy discussion on a yacht, followed by the appearance on deck of a curvaceous blond in a negligee shrieking, 'You'll never have me you pig!' Then the creature dived overboard and started shrieking again when

ABOVE
*Commodore John Cox
Stevens welcomes Queen
Victoria and Prince Albert
aboard his yacht* America
*after the yacht's victory at
Cowes in 1851.*

she realised she couldn't swim. A dinghy carried out a very public rescue and the undressed female slipped away while on the yacht's deck a completely naked man yelled, 'Let the bitch sink!'

Not all the confrontations were so worldly or so trivial. One day in 1866, Mr Lorillard, a tobacco planter and the owner of *Vesta*, and George and Franklin Osgood who owned *Fleetwing*, were discussing the respective performance of their schooners. The discussion became heated enough for them to agree to compare their yachts' speed in a transatlantic race from Sandy Hook to the Isle of Wight. The stake? Each would bet $30,000 for the winner to pocket. They agreed to have no restrictions on the style of rigging and for the competitors to be allowed to make themselves lighter by throwing everything overboard except for the ballast. James Gordon Bennett decided to join in the adventure with *Henrietta*. They were racing for pleasure and for glory.

It was agreed the race would start on 11 December 1866. The three schooners kept to their racing sails and their captains tuned them as much as possible. A wave swept eight men overboard from *Fleetwing* and only two of them were recovered. Within sight of the Scillies, *Vesta* was ahead of *Henrietta* by 40 minutes. *Vesta's* pilot wasn't as successful at negotiating the tidal currents in the race up the Channel and *Henrietta* won in 13 days, 21 hours and 45 minutes. *Fleetwing* had lost a lot of time looking for the men lost overboard but Osgood's very fast yacht had made up the

greater part of their deficit and arrived second, 8 hours and 15 minutes after *Henrietta*. Bennett pocketed the $90,000 thereby acquiring a very flattering notoriety as he was the only owner to have sailed aboard his own yacht. Two new transatlantic races were held. In 1870, *Dauntless* James Gordon Bennett's old yacht, which had been bought by Colt the inventor of the revolver, and *Cambria*, commanded by an old sea dog Captain Tannock, raced from east to west on their way to the United States to fight for the America's Cup. During the crossing they ran short of fresh water but the owner decided, 'It doesn't matter. We can drink the champagne'. This sacrifice wasn't enough though for after a 23-day crossing, *Cambria* won by one hour 17 minutes. There was no further competition across the ocean until 1905 when William II donated the Kaiser's Cup, a gold trophy. Eleven of the best great yachts in the world took part. The smallest was 33 m (108 ft) and the longest 75 m (246 ft). The three-masted *Atlantic*, 56 m (183 ft) in overall length and 40.85 m (134 ft) at the waterline was in the middle of the fleet, but she had an ace master. In charge was Charlie Barr, the best skipper of his time as he had already proved in the America's Cup, and he drove the sailing boat at breakneck speed. One night when the weather was bad, reefing the sails would have seemed to be the right thing to do, but that would have meant not knowing Charley Barr and the discipline and training he gave his crew. The owner and his guests on

their knees in the saloon could only pray as in 24 hours the *Atlantic* covered 631 km (341 nm) miles at an incredible average speed of 14.2 knots and crossed the finishing line off Lizard Point in first place. The three-masted yacht had covered the 5,574 km (3,013 nm) in a record time of 12 days, four hours and one minute. There was a disappointment in store, however, for when the holder of the Kaiser's Cup wanted to melt it down to help in the war effort it was discovered that this goldsmith's piece of work wasn't made of solid gold but was just common plate.

Nevertheless, these exploits didn't mean that the great preoccupation of American yachting was forgotten: that is to keep the trophy won by *America* in 1851, and which symbolised the supremacy of the new America. The nine original yachtsmen of the New York Yacht Club had been joined by hundreds of wealthy, enthusiastic members and each year

Yankee yachtsmen respectfully celebrated its inaugural date of 30 July 1844. By 1880 the club had a thousand members, and between 1884 and 1901 it was based at 67 Madison Avenue, Manhattan in a three-storey brick building which had previously been a school of dance. Then, in 1901 the New York Yacht Club moved into luxurious premises built at 37W 44th Street on land donated by Pierpont Morgan. Even discounting yachts less than 12 m (39 ft) in length the club had 1,565 five members, including 12 women yacht owners. It hadn't been easy for these women to be admitted. One of them was Lucy Carnegie, the owner of *Dungeness* a 36-m (118-ft) steamer. Women members were not allowed into the New York Yacht Club's premises, nor were they allowed to take part in ballots. Their privileges were limited to being allowed to fly the club flag and to use the stations and facilities that the New York Yacht Club had installed in the bays and anchorages that its members visited.

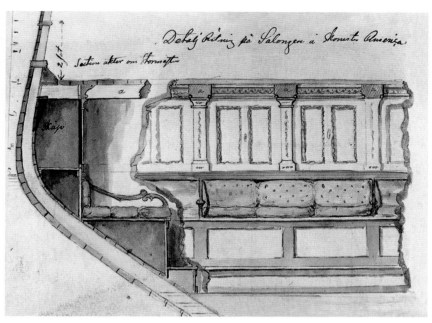

The difficulty of gaining admittance into the club set up by John Cox Stevens and the need for a base closer to other centres of yachting had led to the formation of other yacht clubs, like the Eastern Yacht Club at Boston, whose sailing boats had the reputation of being safer and more seaworthy than those contained within Long Island Sound, the Corinthian Yacht Club, or the Oyster Bay Club, reserved for amateurs. Some clubs were set up on the West Coast, such as the one at San Francisco where the strong westerly winds and powerful tides made sailing difficult. *Casco*, a 26-m (85-ft) schooner that Stevenson chartered for a cruise in the South Seas was one of the most famous yachts in the Bay. The boat, originally owned by Doctor Sam Merritt a multimillionaire from Oakland, then went on to seal hunting in the Arctic and then to the less commendable trades of transporting opium and illegal immigrants from Asia.

Defending the America's Cup was far from the minds of Californian yachtsmen and remained in the hands of those of the East Coast. For a long time Stevens and his friends had called the trophy they had won 'the Queen's Cup' even though Victoria had nothing to do with it. In 1857 Stevens' syndicate gave it to the New York Yacht Club as an international trophy to be called the America's Cup. In the Deed of Gift the donors laid down the rules of the competition. Any organised yacht club from any foreign country would always have the right, through the medium of one or more of their members, to attempt a contest by sail in a match with the Cup as the stake. The document also expressed the wish that the Cup would be the object of 'friendly meetings between the nations of the world'. On 21 July 1857, the New York Yacht Club invited yacht clubs from across the whole world to come and compete for the recently created America's Cup, promising 'a warm welcome and most correct fair play'. However, it wasn't until almost 20 years after the affront inflicted by *America* on British yachting that James Ashbury issued a challenge in the name of the Thames Yacht Club. *Cambria's* victory on the Atlantic crossing of 1870 left no doubt that the British schooner could be a redoubtable adversary. The way to carry out the competition proposed by James Ashbury was the subject of lively debate. As had happened for *America* in 1851, the Yankees required *Cambria* to face a whole flotilla of American yachts. A total of 20,000 spectators watched the first race on 8 August 1870 which took place over a 70 km (38 nm) course between Staten Island and the Sandy Hook lightship and back. Against a fleet of 18 opponents, *Cambria* finished in tenth place behind sailing yachts with lifting keels such as *Magic* and *Sylvie* and was even beaten by the old *America*. The following year James Ashbury had a new, heavily canvassed schooner the *Livonia*, built at Cowes by Ratsey. She had 1,670 m² (17,975 ft²) of sail on a 35-m (115-ft)

ABOVE TOP
A relief of the simple, light fittings of America, *watercolour by Pehr Cedergren.*

ABOVE
The 100-Guinea Cup, renamed America's Cup and nicknamed 'the ugly silver jug'.

FOLLOWING DOUBLE PAGE
Marjorie, *and the 31-m (102 ft) cutter* Galatea, *which was the British challenger in the America's Cup of 1886.*

hull. The conditions of the match provoked new discussions. The challenger, who only wanted to meet his opponents one at a time, threatened to bring so many challenges in the name of so many yacht clubs that they would each have named opponents. The New York Yacht Club asked George Schuler, the only remaining member of the Stevens syndicate to arbitrate. He said that 'a match means that two opponents meet on equal terms'. Cleverly twisting Schuyler's wishes, the New York Yacht Club reserved the right to choose the sailing boat that would face *Britannia* in each of her races. So it was that James Ashbury's heavily ballasted schooner was beaten by 27 minutes in the light north-easterly wind of 16 October 1871 by the sailing yacht with a lifting keel, the *Columbia*. The second race took place at sea in a fresh breeze. *Livonia* won the start and was two minutes in the lead at the first mark. She left it to starboard as was customary in English sailing, but *Columbia* rounded it to port which gave her a clear advantage and a win by ten minutes. James Ashbury's protest was refused as the course instructions didn't state on which side the boats had to pass the mark.

Columbia was beaten in the third race because of rudder problems but in the final two races, a keeled boat, the *Sappho* showed that American yachts were still faster and could sail closer to the wind than the best British schooners.

Two mediocre Canadian challenges then had important consequences for the Cup's rules. The New York Yacht Club accepted that matches would in future be between one challenger and a single defender and again they called on the help of George Schuler to avoid uncompetitive challenges. He decided that only unbeaten yachts and yacht clubs that sailed on the sea would be allowed to challenge, thereby eliminating the Great Lakes' yacht clubs.

It was only in 1885 that the British again thought of recapturing their lost trophy. The Royal Yacht Squadron issued a challenge with Sir Richard Sutton's *Genesta*.

In 1885 it was Edward Burgess,
a young naval architect, who was given the
responsibility of designing the American defender.
He created a 28.65-m (94-ft) yacht with a
centreboard, the Puritan *to face* Genesta.

The challenger was typical of the British yachts of the era. She was 27.45 m (90 ft) long, 4.57 m (15 ft) wide and a real blade of a boat: she needed 70 tonnes (154,323 lb) of lead ballast to balance her lack of breadth and her 650 m² (6,996 ft²) of sail.

Which of the defenders was going to face this champion? The Eastern Yacht Club at Marblehead put their trust in Edward Burgess, a young amateur architect who had studied entomology at Harvard. He designed yachts for pleasure but the largest he had so far drawn up the plans for was only 11.6 m (38 ft) in length.

When he was on holiday in Bristol with his wife in the 1870s Burgess became a friend of the Herreshoff's and being new to yachting had asked to visit their boatyard. He had admired a model of the *Shadow*, appreciated the purity of her lines, and used her as his inspiration for the design of *Puritan*. She was a sloop with a lifting keel, was 28.65 m (94 ft) in length, with a 7 m (23 ft) beam and drew 2.65 m (8.7 ft) increasing to 6.1 m (20 ft) with the centreboard lowered, and was the ship that was selected after the qualifying heats.

A fresh breeze was blowing in the first round, and *Puritan* on the port tack collided with *Genesta*. Very correctly the American yacht was disqualified by the committee, but Sir Richard Sutton didn't want to win in such a way and asked for the race to be re-run. In the light winds of this first race *Puritan* was to be the winner. In the second, with a fresh breeze. *Genesta* was clearly in the lead at the beginning of the leg but she kept too much canvas while her adversary who struck her spinnaker sail and pole caught up the lost time and went on to win by six minutes. Sutton had lost the race but had won the respect of his opponents through his sportsmanship. *Galatea*, which issued the following year's challenge, had the distinction of belonging to a couple who lived on board, a former navy officer, Lieutenant Henn and his wife. Edward Burgess again designed the defender, *Mayflower*, this time for Charles J. Paine who had won his promotion to the rank of general during the War of Succession. Paine had the advantage of a family fortune, which he had increased through a wealthy marriage but his style could scarcely be called elegant, if his contemporaries are to be believed. 'He used to stand on deck with a particularly cumbersome set of binoculars, wearing an old, stained straw hat, a blue flannel shirt and some old trousers with red braces'. But the fact remains that *Mayflower*, helmed by Hank Haff, an excellent captain on the yachts of that period, easily dominated *Galatea*, which was weighed down with all the comforts of a floating home. There was a chance of it all going differently with *Thistle*. Designed by Watson, she was built and launched in the greatest secrecy. The era of the schooners was replaced by that of immense cutters. The brilliant Burgess didn't give the challenger a chance in his creation of the 26-m (85-ft) *Volunteer*. She so clearly dominated the racing that her challenger's owner, James Bell, sent divers down to check that nothing had been attached to the hull to explain the relatively slow pace of his yacht. George Schuyler, by now 76 years old, was again approached, and he produced a third version of the Deed of Gift. From then on the challenger had to give six months' notice, and supply details of the yacht's length and breadth at the waterline, beam, draft and the type of rigging, all of which would allow the New York Yacht Club to provide an opponent of the same

class. The irascible Lord Dunraven was unable to reach agreement with the New York Yacht Club in 1889 on conditions for a meeting, and it wasn't until 1893 that he came with *Valkyrie II*, preceded by the excellent reputation of her architect, George Watson. It wasn't possible to call on the talents of Edward Burgess to defeat her, for after designing 137 yachts, three of which had defended the Cup, the Bostonian was terminally ill. He died at the age of 43, exhausted and a victim of typhoid.

America was lucky enough to find another genius. The young Herreshoffs were making people take note of them. John, 22 years old and blind, sailing their 7.92-m (26-ft) yacht with his brother James as crew, overtook the yacht *Qui Vive* so easily that its owner followed the young men and ordered a yacht from them. During a trip round Europe as a youngster, James had fitted a petrol engine to his bicycle thereby inventing the motorcycle, and in Switzerland, before rejoining his family's boatyard, he had discovered the advantages of having a fixed keel on a sailing boat.
The third brother Nathaniel, who had trained as an engineer at MIT, was also a daring designer and would go on to earn the nickname of the 'Bristol Sorcerer'. In 1891, Nat Herreshoff, practically unknown before, had designed a 21-m (70-ft) cutter, the *Gloriana* for E. D. Morgan. Her design was secret and she won all seven of her races. *Gloriana* was full of innovations. Her overall length was a third longer than her length at the

waterline, her fittings were arranged to concentrate the weight, she was light, with the ballast being 60 per cent of her displacement. After Burgess's death people naturally turned to Herreshoff to design an opponent to *Valkyrie II*. *Vigilant* was built under the greatest secrecy. The hangar doors were kept closed and the windows obscured, but journalists did manage to reveal the defender's construction by dint of spying and taking advantage of careless talk. *Vigilant* was different. She was built in bronze, on a steel frame, moderately ballasted, and with a centreboard in a deep housing. The yacht was far longer than her waterline length. She was 38 m (124.5 ft) overall compared to 26 m (85 ft) at the waterline, and with 1,047 m² (11,248 ft²) of sail, carried 185 m² (1,991 ft²) of sail more than her opponent. *Vigilant* had another advantage too. She had been put in the hands of Charlie Barr. He was a small man who had emigrated from Scotland as a sailor. He was agile, with piercing eyes, black hair and a bushy moustache, and had become the best helmsman and skipper of his generation. On board he imposed an unwavering discipline and trained to perfection his mainly Scandinavian crew of 70 men, who through their strength and effectiveness became known as the 'Norwegian Steam'. He calmly imposed his authority, never losing his dignity as captain, and gave brief and concise orders that his second passed on to the crew. He had the gift of a formidable memory being able to remember the details and tactics from hundreds of races, and knew by heart the instructions, tides and currents for each course.

Added to all this he was a born storyteller who charmed his listeners with tales of his exploits. Despite all the attributes of the American defender, *Valkyrie II* proved herself a disquieting challenger. In the first race, on 5 October 1893, she easily overtook the defender. But the wind dropped and the race was cancelled. Two days later, still in light winds, *Vigilant* won by six minutes and carried off the last two heats, but the margin was so slight that it could be seen that Watson had designed a boat that was as fast as the American defender.

Lord Dunraven returned, full of hope, two years later with *Valkyrie III*. Nothing had been neglected in the design of the cutter that was to face Lord Dunraven's new yacht. In the small nautical world all talk was of the *Vendenese*, a sailing ship built in France from a new, lighter material called aluminium. William K. Vanderbilt and E. D. Morgan joined forces with Oliver Iselin to finance the defence of the Cup. This man with a fierce moustache was born into wealth, and a good marriage had definitely sheltered him from the problems of life. Iselin went to Le Havre specially to see the *Vendenese*. Even if combining aluminium and bronze in the same hull transformed the yacht into a self-destructing stack, the gains justified the risk and the construction would easily last long enough to win a series of races! Herreshoff designed the *Defender*, which had lighter structural hull work and carried more canvas.

This episode in the America's Cup was marked by a series of disputes. After he had lost the first heat Dunraven lodged a protest, claiming that some ballast had been added to *Defender* after her handicap had been calculated. The protest was judged unfounded and was rejected, provoking Lord Dunraven's anger. An undisciplined flotilla of boats carrying some 65,000 spectators came to watch the second race. Just as they were about to start the race, a spectator boat that had ventured close to the line got in the way

of the two yachts and they collided. *Valkyrie's* boom caught in a shroud on *Defender's* top mast, the shroud came away from the cross-trees and the crew had to slow down to stop the top mast from breaking. *Defender* lost the race by 47 seconds but was judged to have been first at the time of the accident. *Valkyrie III* was disqualified in spite of Lord Dunraven's lively protestations. He claimed that at least one of the spectator boats had tried hard to turn his boat from the wind and demanded a clear course, which the committee said would be impossible.

Once she had crossed the start line in the third race *Valkyrie III* turned round and returned to port. Lord Dunraven had abandoned the race, causing an outcry in both the United States and Canada, and in an article published in London's *Field*, he accused the New York Yacht Club of trickery. His bad temper and allegations led to his exclusion from the New York Yacht Club and the 'Dunraven affair' came very close to sounding the death knell for the America's Cup.

To answer the challenge issued by Lipton in 1899, *Columbia* was another of Herreshoff's designs. Oliver Iselin, one of his patrons was on board. He would dedicate ten years of his life to defending the Cup and was always accompanied by his wife Hope who looked after the time keeping and whose advice was invaluable. In 1901 Lipton challenged again. Until then the financial defenders of the Cup had always been members of the New York Yacht Club, but this time a Bostonian came forward as a candidate. Thomas Lawson was a strong character. When he was 12 he left home so as to no longer be a charge on his widowed mother and joined a brokerage company. At 17, he carried out a brilliant transaction on railway shares, but found himself ruined just a few days later. Then by the age of 30 he had a million dollars. He was a puritan against the dissolute morals of New York and called on a local architect, Bowdin Crownninshield. This creator of pretty fin keels was also a womaniser, according to his contemporaries, 'a frenetic, indefatigable sex maniac'.

Lawson's yacht was exclusively Bostonian, designed by a local architect, and built in Boston. The 43-m (141-ft) *Independence* with her enormous overhang, bronze hull, aluminium deck and hanging rudder, suffered from an uncontrolled structure that meant the hull was so flexible that it threatened to cut itself in two. Her disappointing performances meant he had to rely on an improved *Columbia*.

ABOVE
Valkyrie III *and* Defender, *adversaries in the 1895 America's Cup.*

Lipton's wish to use sailing boats of smaller dimensions was linked to a second worry, the desire to race under less ruinous conditions, and the adoption of an equitable handicap system. This everlasting problem had led to the development of more or less successful formulas in both the United States and Great Britain. In 1882, the Seawanake Rule took into account the length at the waterline and the square root of canvas. Burgess designed yachts within the Forty Foot Open Class and Herreshoff designed *Gloriana*, which was in the Forty-Six Foot Class. Something important happened in 1884 when the great yacht, *Victoria's* subsidiary sails proved surprisingly fast and a whole series of identical sailing boats were built. It was the birth of the monotypes. Some of the New York Yacht Club members ordered four similar boats from Herreshoff, the *Rainbow*, *Mineola*, *Virginia* and *Yankee*. These monotypes, the largest that had ever been built, were 21 m (69 ft) at the waterline, 30 m (98 ft) overall, cost $750,000 and needed a crew of 19 to handle them. Their races were fiercely competitive and the skippers and crews so aggressive that it was almost necessary to rebuild the boats at the start of each season's racing. It was the winning of prizes that motivated the crews. The *Virginia* that William K. Vanderbilt insisted on helming was regularly beaten and his crew, deprived of their share of winnings, mutinied and forced the owner to leave the helm to a professional. After four years of racing the monotypes had suffered so much that they were dismantled. Then finally in 1905, a universal handicap system drawn up by Herreshoff was adopted and this made sailing possible on less expensive yachts.

It was all relative. When the Bostonian Frederick J. Brown ordered a schooner from Herreshoff, the 'Sorcerer' made a model of the *Mariette* as he always did before doing the drawings. This 33.3-m (109-ft) splendour, built in the boatyard that at the height of its fame employed a thousand people, was not put in the water till 1915 and her owner kept her for 12 years. Gibson Flanostock approached another architect, Theodore Ernest Ferris. This rich American banker, the founder of a bank and powerful enough to lend the government money wanted to own 'a sturdy boat with a steel hull, fast, comfortable and able to carry enough provisions for several weeks and with quarters sufficient for a large enough crew' for he wanted to go cruising in the Mediterranean. The order led to the launch of the 47.8-m (160-ft) three-masted schooner, the *Shenandoah* in 1902 and in 1904 Flanostock crossed the Atlantic and fulfilled his wish to go cruising. *Shenandoah* was then sold to a German but reclaimed in 1919 as war damages. But by then the time of the proud multimillionaire American yachtsmen had gone for ever.

'You can do business with anyone, but to go boating you must be surrounded only by gentlemen.'
John Pierpont Morgan

Meanwhile in France

Although France had neither the opulence of the new America, nor the maritime traditions of Great Britain during the Edwardian age, she did benefit from the prosperity arising from the industrial revolution which started in the Second Empire and continued during the Third Republic. The English love affair with yachting had started much earlier. In 1820, Joseph Vincent Antressange, a naval officer who had spent ten years in Great Britain, had started to outline how yachting

36. SAINTE-ADRESSE — Nice-Hâvrais — Palais des Régates

might be developed, but didn't manage to complete the job. Yachts from the Royal Yacht Squadron sailed as a fleet to visit Cherbourg in 1824, 1827 and 1831 and then English yachts sailed to Calais in 1836. In 1838, M. Lebaudy, a sugar merchant came back from Cowes and suggested setting up a sailing club at Le Havre. The Société des Régates du Havre (Le Havre Sailing Club) the first sailing club in continental Europe, organised a competition in 1840 for the fastest yachts from Dieppe and England. The painter Isabey was responsible for fitting out one of the competitors, *La Supérieur*. The Société des Régates benefited from some prestigious patrons, like the Prince of Joinville, the third son of King Louis-Philippe who came to take part in the racing in 1843 with his wife and brother, the Duke d'Aumale, on board *Pluton*, a steam corvette. The *Illustration* of

27 August said that 'the races at Le Havre are undoubtedly the most brilliant and the most popular. The proximity of Great Britain allows the English to participate and the ease of access attracts a large number of people living along the Seine from Honfleur to Paris. A considerable floating population of foreigners from all corners of the world and boats of all nationalities bring a cosmopolitan atmosphere to these races that it would be difficult to find elsewhere'. The Société des Régates asked its members for contributions towards building a 25-ton yacht, *L'Avenir* to beat the English sailing boats. Among the subscribers were Horace Vernet, Isabey, Alphonse Karr, Alexandre Dumas the younger and Adolphe Thiers... Hédouin built the yacht, which was 12.6 m (41 ft) long at the deck, in Paris in a boatyard under the bridge at Change. But work was delayed by the revolution of 1848 and *L'Avenir* was launched too late to take part in the racing. Paradoxically she was sold to an Englishman!

'The races at Le Havre *are undoubtedly the most brilliant and the best supported,' commented the* Illustration *of 1844.*

In 1847, the arrival of the railways made it easier for the Parisians and the inhabitants of the Seine valley to get to Le Havre. The following year, Prince Louis-Napoleon became a member of the club and the Bonapartes ordered several yachts from the Augustin Normand boatyards. These were the *Jérome Napoléon*, a 79-m (259-ft) schooner-rigged, propeller-driven wooden boat in 1865, *La Mouche* for Queen Hortense, *L'Abeille* and *Le Lutèce*, and in 1869 *L'Hirondelle* for the Empress Eugénie. However it wasn't until 1863 that the Société des Régates developed its organisation and laid down its regulations. The Emperor came to watch the

sailing in 1867. The following year, some of the great foreign racing schooners *Cambria*, *Sappho*, *Vindex*, *Livonia* and *Niobe* came to Le Havre and raced against Benoit Champy's *Diane*, a lone schooner carrying the French flag. In 1869, a race between Le Havre and Cherbourg saw boats from various categories competing, pleasure boats, pilot boats, and fishing boats. After the 1870 disaster and the creation of the Third Republic, Felix Faure, the Lower Seine region's deputy, became the seventh president of the Société des Régates in 1875.

A little conceitedly the people of Le Havre thought that their competitions could only be equalled by the weeks at Cowes and Kiel. Their view was supported by the sight of the great British 23-m (75-ft) yachts such as *Shamrock*, *White Heather*, and *Nyria* in Le Havre's harbour. During the Universal Exhibition in 1900 there were races between the 20-ton *Esterel*, *Nan*, *Anna* and *Laurea* among others. The clubhouse, built in 1907 due to the generosity of the department store owner, Georges Dufayel, hosted brilliant receptions. Foreign yachts, like that of Alfonso XIII, the King of Spain, took part in the racing. In 1913 the 75th anniversary of the club was celebrated in style. There was an impressive fleet of ships anchored in the harbour, 20 destroyers, three submarines, and five torpedo boats, and 128 yachts from nine

In the second half of the nineteenth century shrimpers and fishing boats *raced alongside the local yachts, at St Malo and at Granville.*

countries took part in the races. The race between Dover and Le Havre for the Edward VII Cup was won by *Haiser*, a German yawl. Raymond Poincaré, the President of the Republic arrived by special train on 22 July to watch the racing. He was very impressed by the quality of the competitors and said, 'living as they must, in the intimacy of the sea, they bring to our race those qualities which are essential for survival'. The evening was crowned with great Venetian celebrations with fireworks and an illuminated cascade.

Activities of French yachtsmen weren't limited to Le Havre. They sailed off all the coasts and had three rivals competing at St Malo for many years, since 1849. Clubs were formed just about everywhere, at Dinard in 1860, St Malo in 1885, Granville in 1889, at Pouliguen and at Nantes. Les Sports Nautiques de l'Ouest (The Water Sports of the West) based at Erdre, was founded in 1882. One of the club's 20-ton yachts *La Rose Friquet* had an

actress as its sponsor, Mme Borgnes, whose attractive bust had provided the model for the Nereid figurehead on the bow. The 6-m (20-ft) JI *Mac Miche* with which the Thubé brothers became Olympic champions at the Stockholm Olympics in 1912 was also a member of Les Sports Nautiques de l'Ouest. The races were bitterly contested at Paimpol, Morlaix and Arcachon in 1854, at La Rochelle in 1860 and at Royan.

One of the members of the Sports Nautiques de la Gironde (Gironde Water Sports) which was set up in 1878, was on the bank watching his yacht through a telescope. He became completely involved in the boat's manoeuvres even though he wasn't aboard, and cried out from the end of the jetty, 'I'm tacking!' Then he turned to the judges, brandishing a handkerchief in place of a flag and said 'I'm tacking under protest!'

The Mediterranean also had top class competitions. One of the first regattas was held in Marseilles harbour on 13 September 1846. Since 1861 the Société des Régates de Marseille (Marseilles Sailing Club) had been the second largest yacht club in France based on the number of boats. It had 55 yachts which was

fewer than Nantes but more than Le Havre and its members met in a floating clubhouse moored in the Old Port, right in the centre of the town. In 1880 a special committee was formed for the Mediterranean races under the patronage of the President of the Republic, the Humbert kings, Alfonso XIII, their Royal Highnesses the Prince of Wales and the Prince of Monaco, and was personally presided over by the Prince of Wales. From 1894 to 1897, prestigious British yachts such as *Britannia*, *Satanita* or *Ailsa* raced against each other at Cannes, Menton, Nice, Marseilles and Sète. The Prince of Plagina, one of the members of Marseilles's 'Nautique' owned a 63-ton yacht, the *Romania*.

Meanwhile, a completely different nautical event was taking place on the Seine. The Parisians who loved boating and sailing congregated in the basin at Argenteuil. The stretch of water benefited from good winds and a lack of strong currents. The Pénaud brothers constructed a boatyard there in 1846, M. Lombard built a house and some villas, and Lucien Môve set up the Société des Régates Parisiennes (Parisian Sailing Club) there in

ABOVE
Dinard 1911–1912, *oil painting by Ethel Carrick Fox (1872–1952).*

FACING PAGE ABOVE
Racing at Granville.

FACING PAGE BELOW
The committee of the Société des Régates du Havre in 1878. In the centre, the president, Félix Faure.

FOLLOWING DOUBLE PAGE
The Cercle de la Voile de Bordeaux racing at Royan in the second half of the nineteenth century, painting by Henry Charles Stock (1826–1895).

ABOVE
*The Mediterranean
hosted top class
international competitions.
Here, the port of Menton
in about 1900.*

FACING PAGE ABOVE
*Yachts of the Société
des Régates Parisiennes
at Asnières in 1855.*

FACING PAGE BELOW
Yachts moored at Asnière.

ABOVE
The jetty of the Cercle de la Voile de Paris built at Argenteuil in 1877.

FACING
The Cercle de la Voile de Paris racing at Argenteuil in 1891.

1853. Trains ran from Paris to Asnières and then one had to continue the journey on foot, but soon the railway was extended as far as Argenteuil reducing the journey time to 22 minutes. Amateurs raced cutters, one of which was the imported American sailing yacht with a lifting keel, the *New York*, and one of the famous sandbaggers which was used as a model for *Lison*, a yacht which measured 7 m (23 ft) on the waterline, carried 112 m² (1,205 ft²) of sail and bags of sand as ballast.

Le Temps of 23 May 1880 commented, 'they have made themselves into an aristocracy. The passion of the Parisians for the countryside is well known, and those who holiday on the banks of the Seine have been joined by those

who holiday on the water. From simple rowing boats their ambitions have grown to sailing boats, some have even gone as far as steam boats, and these pretty sailing boats can cost up to 5,000 francs and a steam boat about 15,000 to 20,000 francs'.

These Parisians were Guy de Maupassant and Jules Michelet and the painters Claude Monet, Auguste Renoir and Gustave Caillebot, who when they weren't taking part themselves, would set up their easels side by side to paint nautical scenes.

In 1868, the Société des Régates Parisiennes became the Cercle de Voile de Paris (the Paris Sailing Circle) and moved into a clubhouse in 1877 at Argenteuil, the first in France. They also had a base in Paris whose atmosphere astonished the *Petit Moniteur's* writer. On 30 May 1883 he wrote, 'as soon as one enters the Cercle's rooms, all one sees is totally nautical, it is the same for what you hear too. These traders, painters, employers, even the lawyers, all these people from different professions normally only talk about the same things: sailing for pleasure, boat building details, rigging, and manoeuvres'.

Gustave Caillebotte, with his young brother Martial, had been one of the most enthusiastic members since 1877. Thanks to their father who held the monopoly for the supply of material and blankets to the army, the brothers enjoyed a life of ease and Gustave Caillebotte was free to exploit all the facets of his genius. As a painter he was a friend of

Dégas, Renoir and Monet and he was also a philatelist, a horticulturist and a talented sailor winning two first prizes with his first boat *Iris*. His *Condor* was built purely for speed and became the fastest boat on the stretch of water due to its 97 m² (1,044 ft²) of white silk sails, which cost the staggering sum of $1,500. He designed a 10-ton yacht, raced at Le Havre and in England and, to be able to compare them, imported a cutter from England, and a sharpie from the United States which was so ugly he christened it *Le Pou* (*The Louse*). He designed a boat with the same measurements as *Condor* and in a deliberately saucy move named her the *Cul Blanc* (*White Bottom*). In 1885 confident in the qualities of his design he challenged M. Brault's *L'Éclaireur* for a 25-Louis stake. The course was to be 25 circuits of the lake, but by 7.50 p.m. *Cul Blanc's* lead was so great that her opponent abandoned the race.

Maurice Chevreux, a talented architect and builder trained at the Augustin Normand boatyard and then in Scotland. He managed a boatyard at Argenteuil that was financed by Gustave Caillebotte. Caillebotte had the idea of fixing lead ballast on the end of a steel plate onto Eugène Lamy's keeled yacht, which had been designed by Chevreux. It was the first bulb-keel to be tried successfully in competition.

In 1890 the members of the Cercle de la Voile de Paris were upset by a plan to build a bridge taking the Paris sewerage to the Achères plains, which would form a barrier blocking their stretch of water. The construction of a railway

PRECEDING DOUBLE PAGE
Women in a sailing
dinghy, *painting by Jules
Cayron (1868–1940).*

ABOVE
*Gustave Caillebotte and
Eugène Lamy, owners of
the first racing yacht to
have a bulb keel.*

disqualified in spite of her opponents' protests. The following day in storm force winds the French defender capsized before the start, and sportingly the *Scotia* abstained from starting. On 15 May, with the wind still extremely strong, *Scotia* attached a storm sail to the yardarm and ran up a 0.6 m² (6.5 ft²) storm gib while *Sidi Fekkar* arrived at the line fully reefed. At the Triel buoy, the French boat was 20 minutes behind but the wind died down, the Cercle's representative shook out his reefs and won by three minutes. Finally, in milder weather *Sidi Fekkar* won the last legs and kept the Cup to the rapturous applause of thousands of spectators. But in 1910 at Kiel the competition between the representatives of seven countries was won by the Danish boat *Agnes II* and the Cup created by the Cercle de la Voile de Paris went abroad.

Gustave Caillebotte, who would later become the vice-president of the Cercle, took part in and won races at Argenteuil and then at Meulan. One day when he was short of a crew member he took on a young painter called Paul Signac. This experience filled Signac with such enthusiasm that he went on to buy 31 boats in succession, became a painter of seascapes and founded the Saint-Tropez Sailing Club. Caillebotte drew up a national handicap system to enable boats to sail on an equal footing that was adopted during a meeting of 25 sailing clubs held at the Yacht Club de France in 1886. Three years later Gustave Caillebotte created a class based on the sail surface area, the 30 Square Metres (323 Square Feet) and the series was extremely successful. He designed seven copies in 13 months, two of them for himself, the *Roastbeef* and *Lézard*. He also designed the 14.8-m (48 ft) *Gloria* for Raphaël G. Prendel of Havana, which won all the races between Cuba and Louisiana. All this activity wore him out and he hardly ever raced again, instead looked after the garden at his Petit-Gennevilliers home and painted only boats and flowers. He stopped collecting stamps but the British Museum later recovered them; today they would be worth some 5 million euros. This painter, architect, horticulturist, sailor, philatelist and patron, who died in 1894 at the age of 46 from a stroke, left an incredible collection of paintings by his impressionist friends.

bridge in 1893 finally forced members of the Cercle move to Meulan and build themselves a new clubhouse.

In 1900 more than a hundred sailing yachts raced regularly on the stretch of water between Les Mureaux and Triel. The sailors travelled to Meulan on the Ouest-État (West-State) Railway in a special carriage with the emblem of the Cercle de la Voile de Paris on the door. Some risked coming by car and Armand Esders caused a sensation by landing a plane on the field at Mureaux.

On the evening of 11 October 1898 at the end of the club members' monthly dinner M. Mantois, the vice-president, announced the creation of a cup for one-ton yachts. Called the One Ton Cup, the trophy was a work of art in solid silver, 10 kg (22 lb) in weight. *Belouga* won the first trials in 1899 against *Vectis* from the Island Sailing Club. The Royal Thames Yacht Club came to challenge the following year with the *Scotia* built to Linton Hope's design. The One Ton Cup was defended by M. Pottin's *Sidi Fekkar* which had been designed by Eugène Laverne, who took turns helming with Vaton depending on the wind. In the first race on 13 May in a fresh north-easterly breeze *Sidi Fekkar* touched a buoy and was

Despite some trials and tribulations the Cercle de la Voile de Paris carried on arranging regattas, and training champions. One such catastrophe occurred in 1910, when the floodwaters of the Seine almost reached the clubhouse roof!

A national authority was needed to oversee the clubs that were springing up everywhere, and a paper to report on their activities. The publication of the magazine *Le Yacht* on 16 March 1878 filled this gap. The previous year on 15 June 1867 the Société d'Encouragement pour la Navigation de

Plaisance (Society to Encourage Boating) was formed under the auspices of the Minister of the Navy, Admiral Rigault de Genouilly, and at the instigation of the Count de Dreuille, the owner of two yachts, *Caprice* and *Satanite*. A few months later the Société d'Encouragement combined with, and took on the name of, the Yacht Club de France under the patronage of the Emperor Napoleon III. The Duke of Villambrosa was elected president and the office passed on the following year to Admiral Rigault de Genouilly. From 1868 all the presidents were either vice admirals or rear admirals until the election of Doctor Jean-Baptiste Charcot in 1913. The Yacht Club de France immediately set out rules defining courtesy and naval etiquette. It cost 100 francs, and an annual renewal fee of 20 francs to obtain a flag, and its accompanying certificate and if yachts failed to fly the flag they would lose their right to membership. These flags were marked according to their owner's rank, four balls and a star for the president, three balls for vice presidents and a single star for

The painters Monet, Renoir and Caillebotte set up their easels alongside each other at Argenteuil to paint nautical scenes.

members. The yachtsman's wardrobe included a dress suit specified down to the smallest detail, as were the insignia and buttons that members were authorised to sew on their blazers. A merger between the Yacht Club de France and the Cercle de Jeux du Pavillon de Hanovre (Hanover Pavilion Sports Club) soon caused problems as there were more sportsmen than yachtsmen. Another society was set up to foster yachting, the Union des Yachts Français (Union of French Yachts) which did much the same as the Yacht Club de France. This association had made a name for itself in 1893 by financing the publication of three books, *Éléments d'astronomie et de navigation* (*Elementary Astronomy and Navigation*), *Construction du Yacht* (*Yacht building*) and a *Guide du Yachtman* (*Yachtsman's Guide*).

ABOVE
Signac in his boat in 1886, *painting by Theo Van Rysselberghe (1862–1926). One day Paul Signac was taken on as a crew member by Gustave Caillebotte. This experience left Signac full of enthusiasm and he went on to buy 31 boats in succession.*

FOLLOWING DOUBLE PAGE
On the yacht, *painting by Pierre Bonnard (1867–1947).*

FACING PAGE TOP
AND BELOW
*Adolphe Demay,
vice president of
the Yacht Club de
France, sailing on
board* Zampa.

ABOVE
*Like most of the
great yacht owning
families, the Meniers
sailed all over the
world. They are seen
here disembarking
at the end of a
cruise.*

PRECEDING DOUBLE PAGE
*Commander Charcot,
a leading member of the
Yacht Club de France
on board* Pourquoi Pas?
*setting sail for the Antartic
in 1908.*

ABOVE
Pourquoi Pas? *breaks
through the last of the pack
ice on her way to the open
sea.*

Finally the Yacht Club de France separated
from the Cercle du Jeux and merged with the
Union des Yachts Français. In 1901 the new
organisation took on the name of Yacht Club
de France and two years later published a
bulletin. During the presidency of vice admiral
Charles Dupéré the members included Edward
VII of England, Alfonso XIII the King of Spain,
the Duke of Montpensier and the Prince of
Monaco. The vice presidents were Adolphe
Demay, the owner of *Zampa*, Arthur Rothschild
and Henri Menier.

The Yacht Club was given state approval
by Raymond Poincaré in 1914. One of its most
eminent members was Doctor Charcot who had
wanted to be a sailor but was made to study
medicine by his father, a famous professor.
The young Jean-Baptiste, however, had tried to
resist his father, and pleaded repeatedly to go to
the baval college asking, 'Marin, Pourquoi Pas?'
(Why not a sailor?), and it became the name
he would give his boats. In 1896 on a 100-ton
schooner built by Fife, the *Pourquoi Pas? (Why
not?)* he went to Shetland and the Faroes.
The second *Pourquoi Pas?* was an 80-ton yacht.
Then in 1903 Charcot was given a grant to
organise a national expedition to Antarctica
to plant the national flag there. He had a
three-masted 32-m (105-ft) schooner, *Le*

Français, built at St Malo. She was manned by
a crew of 20, which included three scientists.
In 1908 she was followed by a new *Pourquoi
Pas?*, 41 m (134.5 ft) at the waterline, in which
Doctor Jean-Baptiste Charcot spent
a memorable winter in Antarctica.
Such were the members of the Yacht Club de
France who met Félix Faure at the offices of
the *Le Yacht* magazine in 1890 to create the
Coupe de France. This was an international
competition for yachts from 5 to 20 tons with
handicaps according to the formula set out by
the Union des Sociétés Nautiques which ruled
over the various clubs and buildings across the
country which displayed their flag. Arthur de
Rothschild gave the promoters the sum of
6,000 francs to buy an objet d'art, a solid silver
trophy weighing 5.7 kg (12.5 lb). The races
were held at Brest and resulted in the selection
of a French representative, M. E. Richard's
20 tonner the 16.4 m (54 ft) *Luciole*. She was
designed and built at Le Havre by Abel Le
Marchand, and won in 1891. E. D. Rothschild's
Bettina was the winner in 1895 but then the
Cup went to England in 1898 with *Gloria's*
victory. Immediately Count Boni de Castellane
started work on the *Anna* which went on to
meet the British defender *Laurea* at Ryde. *Anna*
had to abandon the race because of a damaged
rudder and the Duke Decazes picked up the

torch with *Quand Même* and *Quand Même II*
both of which were built in Bonnin
d'Arcachon's boatyard to plans drawn up by
the famous architect Guédon. *Quand Même II*
brought the Cup back to France when her
English opponent had to withdraw because
she was over the 20-ton limit. In spite of their
success in these regattas and in the Olympic
Games, the French were well aware that they
couldn't compete in the highly charged
symbol of wealth that was the America's Cup.
As Admiral Jurieu de la Gravière said, 'The day
we can challenge for the America's Cup is the
day we will have proved to the world that we
also have that inner strength, the seafarer's
instinct. Winning the America's Cup would
almost be like getting our revenge for both
Aboukir and Trafalgar'.
It was estimated that there were some
thousand yachts of around 20 tons in the
French fleet towards 1890. Measuring boats
and establishing formulas for handicaps
continued to preoccupy all involved in racing.
One attempt at Le Havre classed the sailing
boats according to their length. The French
Register was changed in 1892 and applied
across all of continental Europe and the
number of competitions doubled between
1893 and 1901. One formula used from 1901
tried to equalise the chances of racing yachts
with accommodation, which were likely to
win prizes. In 1891 the Chatou monotype was
created and in 1901 more than a hundred of
them were built, costing 500 francs, at a time
when the price of an 8-m (26-ft) international

handicap was 12,000 francs. The Arcachon
monotype, designed in 1912, had a similar
success and in 1906 the French authorities
adopted the International Register which led
to competitions between 6-m (19.8-ft), 8-m
(26-ft) and 12-m (39 ft) JIs. These tonnage
sailing yachts were elegant and seaworthy but
heavy and costly too. On 19 December 1913
M. de Saint-Père, M. d'Yerre and M. Lenoir
brought together 50 yachtsmen to form the
Union Nationale des Croiseurs, to organise
offshore racing.

Despite the existence of talented naval
architects and skilled boat builders in France,
the British had cornered almost all of the
French market in the great yachts. Fashion
underlined by snobbery and convenience led
many yachtsmen to buy their boats in Great
Britain, as did Baron Sède who bought *Léontin*
in England in 1890. The yacht was then the
first to be put in Le Havre's Carnot basin, which

The young Jean-Baptiste Charcot,
whose father had decided he was to be a doctor,
used to repeatedly ask his father
'Marin, Pourquoi Pas?' (Why not a sailor?) ...
It was the name that he would later give to his boats.

Normand was an exceptionally brilliant naval architect. He was self-taught, curious about everything, passionate about mathematics and astronomy, and designed some outstanding pilot cutters, the Hirondelles de la Manche (The Channel Swallows). In 1895 he designed and built a destroyer which reached the world record speed of 31.02 knots. Then, three years later he conceived and constructed the *Gitana II*, a propeller-driven yacht, 37 m (121 ft) at the waterline which her owner Baron Adolphe de Rothschild took to Lake Geneva where he reached a speed of 26 knots.

One of Jacques Augustin Normand's most remarkable successes however was the delivery of *Zemajteij* in 1876. Although many French yachtsmen ordered their boats from Great Britain, a young Polish count ordered his from France. Baron Benoît Tyszkiewicz was 7 years old and lived in Nice when his mother died. He had never known his father or his grandfather, but had inherited an immense stretch of land and a chateau, the Manoir Rouge, which had burnt down in 1831 and then been rebuilt in the height of luxury. The wealthy young man liked travel and adventure and when he was 21 went to the United States where he met and married Clara Elizabeth Bancroft a 17 year old from a family of shipowners who loved yachting. Benoît Tyszkiewicz who loved France was exasperated by the self-importance of American yachtsmen so he placed an order with a Le Havre boatyard for a yacht with the ability to rival the American schooners. His plan was to go on a world tour and the Polish count was 24 when *Zemajteij* (Lithuanian for 'people of the Low Countries') was launched.

The yacht designed by Jacques Augustin Normand was 42.27 m (138.7 ft) overall, 37.97 m (124.5 ft) on the waterline, schooner rigged and carried 958 m² (10,312 ft²) of Ratsey and Lapthorn canvas. Her wide, flat hull was copied from American boats. In addition to the cast iron interior ballast was 27.5 tonnes (60,627 lb) of lead ballast. Giving the hull a triple skin was an innovative idea and from her first outing she displayed three remarkable qualities: her speed of 16 knots, the way she rode the waves and her ability to sail exceptionally close to the wind.

The young Polishman's yacht was run by a Russian crew managed with military discipline. One of their first cruises took her owners to the Mediterranean and the Black Sea but then in 1877 Clara wanted to return to the Manoir Rouge and her son. *Zemajteij* was taken back to Le Havre and put up for sale. It took two years before a buyer was found, but in 1879 the Baron Roissard du Bellet bought her for 75,000 francs. He was 43, very wealthy and a widower, a former banker, a deputy for the Alpes-Maritimes and had hardly ever been sailing. One day for want of anything better to do he visited the *Zemajteij* at Le Havre and said

had just been completed at a cost of 60 million francs. In the same year J. E. Gauthier, a member of the Yacht Club de France, became the new owner of *M'Aza*, a 26-m (85-ft) schooner built by Ratsey. The 30-m (110-ft) steam yacht *Olbie* bought by R. Le Berthe in 1886 was a Watson design and the same was true of *Vanda*, Mr de Guebriand's 62-ton schooner built in England, Achille Fould's steam yacht, *Bijou* and Arthur de Rothschild's 75-m (246-ft) steamer which employed a crew of 75 and was known for its luxurious fittings with a saloon, bedroom, smoking room, drawing room and six guest cabins. The banker also owned a smaller boat, the *Passe Partout* only 24 m (78.7 ft) in length which he later sold to the American, James Gordon Bennett. Luckily some like Doctor Charcot and also the Count de La Vaux who ordered his 13.75-m (45-ft) cutter, the *Dora* from St Malo, did still place their trust in the French boatyards.

In Le Havre in particular there was a whole generation of exceptionally good designers and builders. The people of Normandy had been shipwrights since the eighteenth century first at Honfleur then at Le Havre where they moved in 1808. At the end of the nineteenth century, one of their descendants, Jacques Augustin

'we were half tempted to gain a fuller experience of the sea'. His son was full of enthusiasm and the expert they consulted said that, 'this little construction has many good nautical qualities and I wouldn't hesitate to say that she was very well built'.

The schooner was given the new name of *Velox*, and re-equipped under the command of Jacques-Eugène Flambart, an ocean-going captain who selected the crew. The boat set sail on 24 October 1879. On board were 32 people, the owner and his son with some English friends and their daughters, Jean's Greek teacher, a chambermaid, two servants and a chef. The schooner called at Plymouth so the passengers could take part in some hunting, then set off south. They had to put up storm sails because of strong winds but the boat handled perfectly. On 26 December there was a sudden squall when they were leaving Gibraltar. 'We were in sight of a sailing yacht that we knew was *Ianira*, an English yacht following the same route as ourselves. We saw her at 7 a.m., 4 miles upwind of us and by 10 a.m. we had left her out of sight downwind'.

Velox's arrival in Nice on 14 January 1880 should have given her the chance to show her mettle in the first races between the best English yachts, but Eugène Roissard lost his

mother in February and decided to go on a cruise. He stopped off at Menton, Gêne, Civittavecchia and Naples where he could have raced against several English yachts, which were also visiting. But *Velox* carried on, covering 109 nm in eight and a half hours, visiting Greece and Turkey before returning to her home port. 'If I had any regrets on my return to Nice, it was that my business affairs meant that I had to leave behind this free, carefree life, the good life'. Going sailing had other attractions for the deputy as it gave him a 'legitimate motive for abandoning thankless politics'. Further journeys took *Velox* into the North Sea and to Scotland. In 1887 Jean Roissard du Bellet, the son whose childish enthusiasm had persuaded his father to buy *Zemajteij*, married Elizabeth Rodgers the daughter of the English friends who had sailed with them in 1879, but *Velox* had been sold the previous year. Her new owner was Henri Seiber, an industrialist from the north of France, originally from Switzerland, who ran a textile mill at Cateau-Cambrésis. Henri Sieber had had an austere childhood in a protestant family and moved straight into work, never marrying. Both he and his brother dreamed of escaping the constraints of an extremely rigid way of life. The youngest, Frédéric, bought a large tract of land in Dinard, built four houses there for the different members of his family

ABOVE
Henri Sieber and his wife on board Velox.

FACING PAGE ABOVE AND BELOW
Velox *in dry dock, and the man who created her, Jacques Augustin Normand. The Normand family was granted the name of Augustin-Normand by a decree issued in 1911.*

and had the steam yacht *Gabrielle*, built. sailed her to the Mediterranean and to the north where he visited Stockholm and Saint Petersburg. In 1887 the two brothers sold most of their shares. Henri bought the *Velox* and yachting became his life-long passion. He became a member of the Cercle de la Voile de Paris and of the Yacht Club de France. *Velox* was given a new set of sails and went to Cowes where she was refitted at Atkey's. She sailed to Scotland, Portugal, Madeira, the Canary Islands, and North America. In 1888 Henry bought the steamer from his brother and owned the two yachts. He led a quiet life. A friend, Émile Reverdin, joined him for some enjoyable sailing on the *Velox* and a trip across the Atlantic was planned for 1897. An American schooner, the *Fleur de Lys* was also due to leave Le Havre at the same time. It was to be a transatlantic race and would certainly have enabled the French yacht to prove her mettle, but George Lord Day changed his departure date to wait for a guest to arrive and Henri Sieber didn't want to alter his programme. *Velox* set sail for Madeira and made an average 11 knots in the trade winds. Reverdin said 'A steam boat that was following the same route as us wanted to pass across our bows, but by the time we had sailed side by side for half an hour, she gave up and crossed astern. Near the Azores on the return journey the wind was fierce. As Émile Reverdin remembered in *Le Yacht*: 'Despite violent winds and huge waves *Velox* performed perfectly and her deck was only occasionally covered with spray. We ate in the dining room as usual as *Velox* passed easily and smoothly through the turbulence'. In 1901, Henri Sieber had a more

modest ketch the *Vizir* built at La Richardais to go sailing in Brittany and used both her and the *Velox* from then on. In 1913 at 70 years of age he went for his last cruise and died. Frédéric who inherited the two yachts put them up for sail. M. Michaud, a Le Havre scrap merchant bought *Velox* and dismantled her. The wood was found to be as sound as when she was first built.

So ended the *Velox* which was the pride of French yachting and which, if she had competed against the yachts built in America and Britain would in all likelihood have confirmed Jacques Augustin Normand's talent to have been at least as great as that of Watson, Fife and Herreshoff.

Velox's amazing career doesn't mean that she was the only yacht under the French flag to have been a great success. Edmond Blanc visited Canada on *Nubienne* as Paul Saunière, one of his guests, later confirmed. The three Menier brothers, industrial chocolate producers, were also determined yachtsmen. Henri was mad about sailing. He studied naval architecture, construction, sail-making, designed small boats and then *Le Sphinx*. In 1881 he sailed around Europe on board *Surrirella* as far as Spitzberg, and also in Asia. He bought the *Nubienne*, renamed her the *Velléda* and sailed to the ice floes. He visited Quebec on board the 62-m (203-ft) *Bacchante*. At the same time he also owned a steamer *L'Almée* for sailing on rivers and estuaries. *La Julie*, Gaston Menier's 100-ton steamer reached speeds of up to 15 knots and Albert ventured all the way to Japan on board the *Némésis*. Étienne Fould's 49-m (160-ft) three-masted

schooner the *Sans Peur* was very luxurious. The main saloon was 6 m² (64.5 ft²), the owner had his own suite of rooms, a smoking room and six guest cabins. He not only went to Iceland, Norway and Lapland but also to Malta, Greece and Turkey too. Eugène Pérignon was one of the most renowned yachtsmen. He was one of the first at L'École central (the Central School), wealthy, and for his own amusement designed his own steamboat the 18.5-m (60.7-ft) *Croissy-Vernon*, and then a longer 26-m (85 ft) version. However, he asked Benjamin Norman to design the 38-m (125-ft) propeller driven *Fauvette*, which took all the honours on two separate occasions. She towed James Ashbury's *Cambria* at the inauguration of the Suez Canal in 1869. Then in 1875 the liner *Normandie* went aground in the Lerin Islands. The weather was atrocious and no one dared to go to the rescue of the shipwrecked passengers and crew. *Fauvette* was at Cannes and Eugène Pérignon gave the order to set sail, took the helm himself and saved the lives of 400 people. He went cruising in the Red Sea as well as up to the north, to Trondheim and Saint-Petersburg. Arthur Rothschild was another enthusiastic sailor. He went to Constantinople on board the 200-ton *Stella*. At a later date he also had the 310-ton *Éros* and the *Éros II* a 75-m (246-ft) steam-sail yacht which he used for cruising in Europe. M. L. Lebeau sailed

around the world undamaged on a 60-m (197-ft) steam-sail yacht the *Apache*, going by way of India, China, the Pacific, the Fiji Islands and the Magellan straits. The members of the literary set sailed as well, in 1867 Jules Verne bought a sailing launch, which he called the *Saint Michel*. The *Saint Michel II* built by Abel Marchand in 1874 was a 20-ton cutter. In 1880 the writer bought *Saint Joseph* a steam-driven schooner from the Marquis de Préaux which was later named *Saint Michel III* and Guy de Maupassant's *Bel Ami* was an English-built 14.6-m (48-ft) yawl.

The accounts of some of these sailors, printed, illustrated and richly bound, make some of the best reading in the wealthy library of the Yacht Club de France. In 1900 according to Philippe Daryl's *Le Yacht*, the French sailing fleet had 1,049 yachts, including 47 schooners, 77 yawls, 588 cutters or sloops, which employed 3,500 crew members. Steam yachts accounted for only a third of all the yachts. A 100-ton schooner then cost between 80,000 and 100,000 francs, and the crews' salaries were then to be paid above that. A captain was paid 250 francs per month, a watch-keeper 200 francs and a sailor 160 francs. Most of the sailors were fishermen and increasingly the amateurs tried to pit themselves against the professionals whose livelihood lay in the skills they required.

ABOVE
Henri Menier on board Bacchante, *on the return journey from Quebec admiring fox pelts caught during the cruise.*

FOLLOWING DOUBLE PAGE
On board his yacht in 1905 the Duke of Orléans spent time taking photographs to bring back as souvenirs of his cruise.

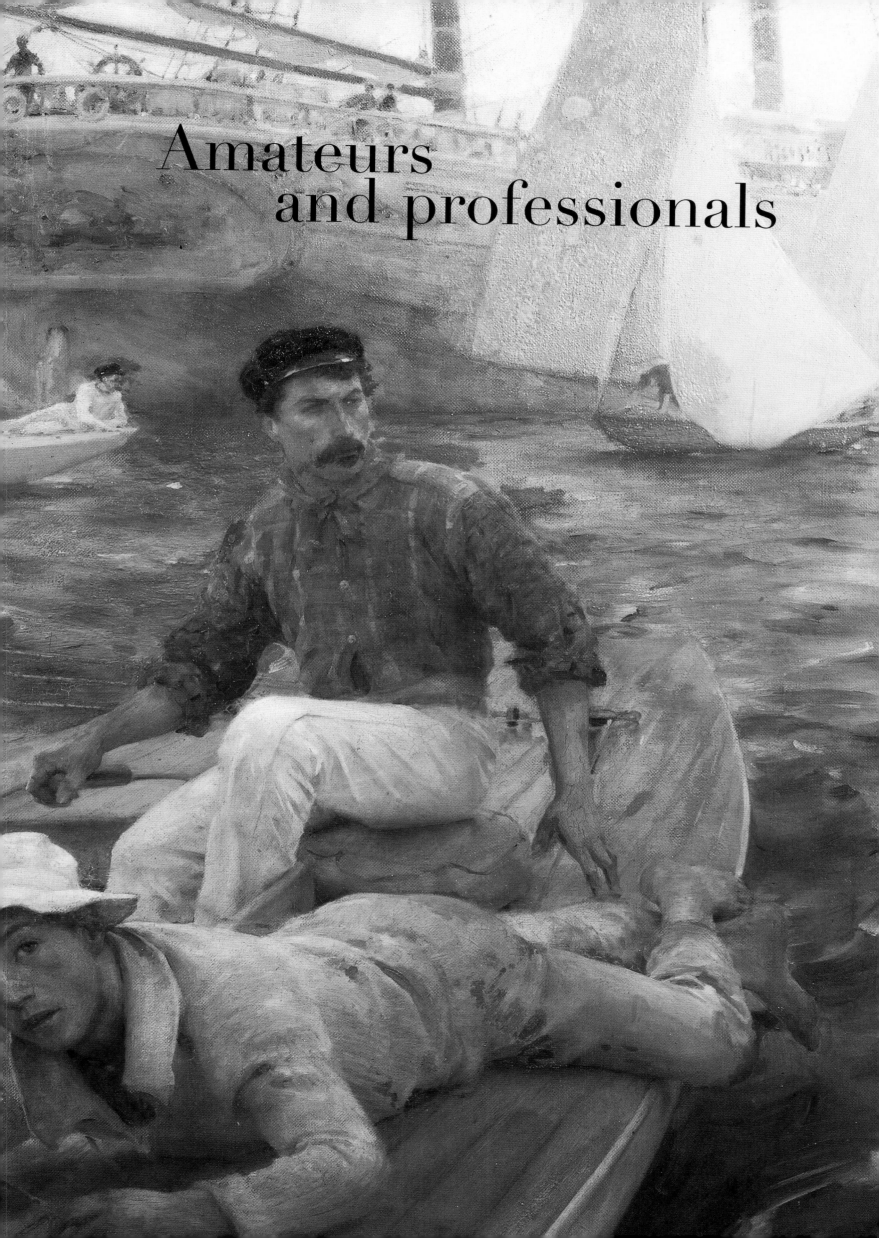

Amateurs
and professionals

PRECEDING DOUBLE PAGE
The last tack, painting by Henry Scott Tuke (1858–1929).

FACING
Luciole off Gibraltar in 1892 on her way from Le Havre to join the racing at Nice.

The great yachts of the Edwardian age were often commanded by captains who had been trained on commercial clippers, and were manned by professional crews so the owner was simply a passenger on his own yacht. Sometimes he wasn't even on board during competitions as happened when *Vesta* and *Fleetwing* were competing in a transatlantic race. Lipton too stayed on his steamer while his yacht *Shamrock* was challenging for the America's Cup.

The sailors, most of them fishermen

*Winning races brought cash bonuses, often £1 per man.
These sums of money made all the hard work worth while.*

chosen by their skipper, were often from the same port or the same area. The preferred crews on the large American racing yachts were the Scandinavians as they were strong, well disciplined and used to terrible conditions. Professional crews took great care maintaining their yachts, they would be up at 5.30 a.m. to scrub the decks and polish the brass before breakfast. It took several hours to get a boat ready for a competition, to make the sails fast to the yardarms and to set the running rigging. All this care was demanded for two reasons. One, the pride of the skippers who made it a point of honour that the yachts they commanded should be impeccable, and two, in their own self-interests, for victory in a race brought a cash bonus, often in England a pound per man. In the course of a season

a good yacht could win up to £1,000 in prize money. These sums of money made the extremely hard work worth while, as Sir Philip Hunloke, an amateur skipper of the royal yacht *Britannia*, said, 'I have raced with and against many professionals. Gomez, Ben and Bill Parker, Sycamore, Charles Beavis and Mountfield were all excellent sailors but I think that Sycamore was the most intelligent. Professionals are often criticised for rushing after an immediate advantage without taking an overall view of the race and I think that is true. If they took time to think, they would not luff an opponent to eliminate them from the race, if it led to their own elimination too. Too often they give in to the temptation to put their nearest competitors out of the running without thinking of the consequences for the rest of the contest. During races they don't use a great deal of imagination and often lose in spite of their vast experience'. Hunloke was

doubtless referring to a manoeuvre from which he benefited from time to time. Almost without exception contestants gave way to the royal yacht even if they had the right of way, and those who didn't observe to this mark of respect were in the eyes of their peers committing the crime of *lèse-majesté*. Sir Philip Hunloke had been a member of the royal yacht Squadron from an early age. He was imbued with aristocratic principles and was a capable tactician, however, he was honest in recognising the qualities of the professional sailors and very aware of the signs of the weather. 'He was aware of any changes in the direction or strength of the wind well in advance, which perhaps amateurs would not normally have noticed and he would change his route to take advantage of it'. If amateurs on board racing yachts didn't have Philip Hunloke's skill, their presence was justified by the need for them to sign the finishing declaration at the end of the race, which stated, on their honour, that the yacht had not infringed any rules and that it had completed the course. According to an amateur skipper this couldn't be done by 'deceitful' professional skippers.

No matter how gifted these amateurs may have been they didn't do the more menial tasks, as Captain Coffin said, 'it is quite normal for guests to pull on the sheets every now and then but it would be absurd to ask them to clean the deck, polish the brass or handle the sails all day'. And even if the best of them like William K. Vanderbilt liked to take the helm, the crew would rebel and take over the running of the yacht, as they were always keen to win the race and take their share of the prize money.

One example of the professionals' work on board comes from 1880 with the amazing careers of the sailors from Dourduff, a tiny fishing port in the Bay of Morlaix. Because of the size of families at that time, the youngsters had to leave the area to find work. Many went to Le Havre, an active centre for yachting, and some were employed on racing yachts. Because of the distance between their harbour and the fishing grounds and the difficulties posed by the rocks and currents in the Bay of Morlaix, the sailors from Dourduff were traditionally skilled at boat-handling. They reacted very quickly to avoid the eddies caused by a reef and the actions of currents and changes in

ABOVE
*As seen here on board
Britannia the amateurs
would lend a hand when
hoisting sails or hauling
in sheets.*

DOURDUFF. - Le Port

tide and weather. From 1880 on, the Dourduff sailors competed in the racing in the Bay of Morlaix on 15 August between fishing boats and such sailing yachts as M. de Kersauson's *l'Hébé*. Yacht owners like Eugène Pérignon, a distinguished yachtsman and one of the directors of the Yacht Club de France, and Georges Pilon winner of a number of the great series of races, appreciated all the skills of these fishermen who had moved to sailing yachts. Henri-François Le Reguer was put in charge of Pérignon's steam yacht *Linnet*, and François Michel in charge of *Henriette*, George Pilon's

cutter built to Fife's plans. Both skippers were originally from Dourduff and so naturally they took on deckhands from their own region. At that time ordinary sailors were paid 50 francs a month, and skippers 80 francs in addition to their clothing and food.

It was Jean Féat who unquestionably had the most successful career of all the Dourduff seamen. He was taken on as a cabin boy on *Fauvette* in 1878 when he was 12 years old, and then became a sailor on *Henriette*. In January 1893 he was a watchmaster on board the *Luciole* which had won the Coupe de France for the two previous years. In 1895 L. Viton had a new yacht built, a 10-ton fin-keeler, the *Luciole II* which was 16.4 m (54 ft) at the deck and 11 m (36 ft) at the waterline. Jean Féat as her skipper won race after race, seven first prizes in 1895 and 15 in 1896. *Luciole III* which was ordered from Le Havre by Abel Le Marchand and launched in 1897 was a 20 tonner, measuring 22 m (72 ft) overall and 15 m (50 ft) at the waterline. Jean Féat's brother was his second-in-command on this boat and once the yacht was finely tuned it won 23 first prizes. By the time he was 33, Jean Féat had become one of the best French helms and it was he who was asked to take charge of the 20 tonner *Esterel*, Maurice Chevreux's design for the 1898 Coupe de France. England and France were neck and neck with one win each, but in the last leg *Esterel's* bobstay broke and she finished up losing by 15 seconds!

A four-year stint in command of the 92-ton steamer *Linotte* followed, but then his passion for sailing again caught hold of Jean Féat.

Dourduff, a modest fishing village in the Bay of Morlaix, became the breeding-ground for the best yachtsmen who snapped up victories from Nice to Kiel.

A committee had fitted out the 10-ton *Armen* to try to win back the Coupe de France that was in the hands of the Germans. The competition took place in Kiel in 1907 and *L'Éclaireur du Finistère* didn't think it out of place to use the headline 'Dourduff versus Germany'. Just as *Armen* was about to win a race the sailor was commanded by its owner to, 'Give me the helm!' but Jean Féat replied 'No! I'm keeping it!' He came in first and won the Coupe de France back from Germany. After *Armen's* victory, *La Dépêche* was full of praise for 'Dourduff's victory'. The people of the little Breton port were deliriously happy, the houses were decked with flags and the inhabitants spent two days celebrating. Jean Féat and his companions were given a heroes' welcome and presented with a national flag embroidered with the inscription 'Gloire et Honneur à Jean Féat' (Honour and Glory to Jean Féat).

Alfonso XIII, the King of Spain, hired Féat to helm the royal yachts, the 10-m (32-ft) JIs *Corzo* and *Tonino*. His brother Vincent helmed *Encarnita*, which belonged to the Marquis of Cuba, one of the King's close relatives. One day in 1910, the two brothers were racing against each other. At one point *Encarnita* was to starboard and Vincent wanted to make use of his right of way. Jean tried to intimidate his brother saying, 'Vincent bear

away, the King is here'. 'No chance,' came the reply, 'I'm the starboard boat!' 'I'm telling you I've got the King on board,' he insisted. 'The King my foot! If you don't tack I'm going to cut you in two'. Fortunately their conversation was carried out in Breton as Jean Féat used a particular strategy to win races. He would shout his orders loudly in French, but his crew would only follow the orders he gave in Breton. In 1911 *Tonino* had to go to Cowes to take part in some racing. On the way Jean Féat decided to stop off in his own country to pick up water and provisions. The inhabitants were amazed to see a yacht flying the Spanish king's flag moored in front of the Café du Port. Once in England the Dourduff sailors won two regattas and Jean Féat stayed in Alfonso XIII's service until 1914. During the 1910 English season Vincent also helmed Philippe de Vilmorin's 8-m (26-ft) JI and carried off seven wins compared to the four wins of the best English boats in this class. The pride of Dourduff, Vincent was given the Croix de Chevalier de la Légion d'Honneur (the Cross of the Chevalier of the Legion of Honour).
Jean-Marie Beuzit, another one of Dourduff's sons, had been trained by Jean Féat and became the skipper of Jean Lose's 8-m (26-ft) JI *Loisir* in 1909. The yacht took 14 first prizes and six second prizes out of 24 races.

ABOVE
The yachts Malgré Tout,
Luciole *and* Samphir
racing at Nice in 1897.

BELOW
*The naval architect
Maurice Chevreux
designed the 20-ton*
Esterel *for the Coupe
de France which was
entrusted to Jean Féat.*

FACING PAGE, ABOVE
*Thomas Lipton's crew
on* Shamrock's *deck.*

FACING PAGE BELOW AND
FOLLOWING DOUBLE PAGE
*Alfonso XIII, a passionate
amateur, took part in the
1910 Cantabrian Cup
races on board his yacht*
Hispania. *The Sovereign
stood alongside his sailors
to acknowledge the cheers
celebrating his victory.*

After the war, Jean Féat, his son Albert, his brother, his nephew and the other hands from the Bay of Morlaix continued to display their talent, their skill and at times their difficult temperaments. During the racing between 24 8-m (26-ft) JIs at Saint-Jean-de-Luz in 1930, Jean Féat was helming *Vim* when her owner suddenly decided to take the helm. It needed all of Jean's son Albert's energies to make him give up his place to Charles Prince otherwise the owner's lack of ability meant they risked

losing the race. Alfonso XIII, who was helming *Hispania*, started rounding the buoy, and Jean Féat was unable to stop himself from shouting furiously at the Sovereign 'Don't poke your nose in!' During some races at Villefranche Albert Féat and his cousin Jean Messager hatched a plan to make a mess of a manoeuvre and slow down the yacht helmed by Jean Féat just as she was about to win the race. The skipper was furious 'What are you doing? Have you forgotten how to handle a boat?' When they had finished Albert explained 'Listen, Dad, didn't you see the programme? First place wins the cup but second place wins 1,000 francs!'

The tradition continued after the war when Dourduff sailors were to be found on yachts belonging to M. Lesieur and Virginie Hériot. In 1965, four strong young lads from Carantec, opposite Dourduff, formed the professional crew of Baron de Rothschild's *Gitana* and once more a 27-m (88 ft) yacht was moored at the slipway at Carantec just as the King of Spain's yacht had previously been seen moored in the port of Dourduff.

The Kaiser and
other royal yachtsmen

The first German yacht club was founded at Königsberg on 7 January 1855. German rulers took up yachting to foster an interest in the sea in their country, as Germans didn't have the same affinity with the sea as the English did. In 1858 the Prussian King Frederick-Wilhelm placed an order with the Augustin Normand boatyard for a three-masted, schooner-rigged, steam yacht which would be capable of averaging 16 knots on the journey between Le Havre and Cherbourg. On 7 June 1868 on a

THIS PAGE
*The bedroom of the
German Empress,
Augusta Viktoria,
on board* Hohenzollern.

FACING PAGE
*The German imperial
yacht in Kiel Canal,
which links the North
Sea to the Baltic.*

superb spring day, the Berliners went to the banks of the Spree to watch the first regatta to be held in the city. Wooded hills alternate with sandy plains to form a natural amphitheatre, ideal for nature-loving spectators. Thirty-five sailing yachts took part, those in the great class carrying 400 m^2 (4,305 ft^2) to 450 m^2 (4,844 ft^2) of sail. There was fierce competition right up to the last tack between a contestant from Potsdam and a boat from Berlin. *Albatross* came first winning this memorable competition by just one minute.

For the Kaiser prestige and diplomacy were the most important aspects of yachting and so he had the *Hohenzollern* built by the North German boatyards at Kiel. She was an 81.6-m (267.7-ft) steel-hulled paddle steamer whose powerful engines gave her a speed of 16 knots and it was on board her that the Kaiser prepared to receive the Tsar. The meeting was scheduled to take place at Danzig at 6 a.m. on 9 September 1881. Wilhelm I the King of

Prussia and Emperor of Germany, accompanied by the Crown Prince, had come from Berlin and went on board his yacht. Chancellor Bismarck and his son arrived shortly afterwards with some staff from the Russian embassy. The German yacht was surrounded by warships and the whole affair was more a matter of protocol than sailing, judging by everyone's clothes. The Kaiser was wearing formal Russian dress decorated with the Order of Saint Andrew and the Cross of Saint George, the Crown Prince was in the uniform of his Russian regiment and Bismark was in a cavalry regiment uniform decorated with all his medals as well as a row of Russian medals. They were ready to receive Tsar Alexander III who was also coming on his yacht, the *Dershawa*, but fog made navigation difficult and *Dershawa* didn't arrive until midday. The Tsar was taken to *Hohenzollern* as soon as possible and climbed the accommodation ladder.

The Russian ruler was also in full formal dress. He was wearing the uniform of the Brandenburg Uhlans with the ribbon of the Order of the Black Eagle. The two Sovereigns greeted each other warmly and *Hohenzollern* flew the flags of both her guest and her host. A special train took them to Danzig but the planned festivities there were ruined by terrible weather and the Tsar left on board the *Dershawa* the morning after this meeting that was diplomatic rather than sporting.

*The German Emperor wanted to be on
an equal footing with the might of British.
yachting for the Kaiser it was first and
foremost a matter of prestige and diplomacy.*

The first Kiel regatta was held in that same year of 1881. Saefkow, a marine engineer had arrived there with his yacht *Anna* in 1880 and on 1 September 1881 a competition was held between *Anna*, *Teifun*, *Adler* and the *Uskan* which Saefkow had built for Prince Frederick-Charles of Prussia. Kiel Bay was well suited to inshore racing and in 1882 more races were held there. Invitations were issued and the best sailing yachts from Hamburg completed the races on 23 July 1882.

129 *The Kaiser and other royal yachtsmen*

Wilhelm II, *Victoria's grandson, was the real champion of German yachting.*

ABOVE
Kaiser Wilhelm II in
foul weather gear on
board his yacht, Meteor II,
in 1910.

FACING PAGE
The first Meteor,
formerly Thistle,
painted by
Hans V. Peterden
(1850–1914).

The weather was glorious and 20 contestants started under the control of the racing committee on board the *AugustaViktoria.* Some 600 spectators arrived on a special train from Hamburg and the Naval authorities were poised for action. All the vessels, ships, boats and small craft had taken to the water to join in the racing, the success of which led to the decision to organise an annual competition, with the active support of the Imperial Navy and the naval officers on board the sailing yachts. Prince Henry raced on *Nelly* in 1885 and the following year the Navy had four 20-ton yachts, *Lust, Liebe, Wille* and *Wunsch* built.

The true champion of German yachting

was Kaiser Wilhelm II who succeeded his grandfather Wilhelm I in 1888. He was Queen Victoria's grandson and dreamt of equalling the prestige and success of the British boats. He unhesitatingly employed English captains and sailors to enable him to build his own team

following the best Cowes traditions. He set up the Kaiserhichter Yacht Club in 1887 with himself as commodore. German yachtsmen took great pride in belonging to this club, sailing became an affair of state and everyone knew that the Kaiser was keen to take the helm himself during his holidays. The Kaiser wanted to put the German fleet at the forefront of all the sailing countries and the imperial yacht had its own contribution to make. In 1891 Wilhelm II bought one of the world's most prestigious yachts, the *Thistle.* She had been built to a Watson design by a group of Scots and put up for sale after her failure to win the America's Cup. Some 90,000 marks or £4,500 must have changed hands. The British press commented on the treachery involved in allowing one of the flowers of the British fleet to pass into foreign hands. *Fairplay* revue wrote, 'it appears that the Kaiser, who is a member of the Royal Yacht Squadron, intends to pay tribute to his annual regatta with a yacht

of the highest quality. Unfortunately, *Thistle* will not be able to participate because she had not been entered by the required date'. The Emperor secured the services of Captain Duncan who retained his own British sailors, while the Germans were in the personal service of the new owner. At the same time a 23.45-m (77-m) yacht, the *Irene*, was being built in Glasgow to a design by Watson for Prince Henry of Prussia, a brother of the Kaiser and a member of the Royal Yacht Squadron. *Irene* was conceived and built purely for racing. Her hull was a composite of steel and teak, her mast and boom was of Oregon pine and she carried 314 m² (3,380 ft²) of sail cut by Ratsey and Lapthorn. *Thistle*, under her new name of *Meteor* arrived in Kiel on 1 July 1891 and the Kaiser went to meet her on the frigate *Grief*. The warships were dressed overall. The *Meteor* appeared over the horizon in the middle of a huge fleet of enthusiastic spectators, sailing at high speed and showing the characteristic speed and elegance of this impressive 30-m (110-ft) yacht with its 1,225 m² (13,186 ft²) of sail and 27-m (88 ft) boom.

The 1892 regatta promised to be a grand affair: the Imperial Yacht Club had 505 members and 50 boats, and the enthusiasm of the imperial family gave added impetus to German yachting. Sadly, the weather was terrible on 29 June when the cannon sounded the 10 a.m. start for 32 yachts. The Kaiser, Prince Henry and the Grand Duke of Mecklenburg were all on board *Irene*. The yachts found it difficult to make headway as the wind strengthened and they were heeling by 40° with their sails soaked half way up the masts. The Emperor and the Grand Duke had donned oilskins, but Prince Henry was in his shirtsleeves at the helm of *Irene*, the leading yacht. The yachts seemed to be sailing in the water as much as on it. *Argo*, one of the smaller contestants sank and her crew had to be rescued. *Lust* and *Wunsch*, sailing alongside each other, collided and *Wunsch* sank quickly. *Troll* called for assistance, the Berlin boat *Vielliebehen* lost her mast, and *Krabble* ended up on the beach. *Irene* won this dramatic race coming in three-quarters of an hour ahead of the second boat *Atlanta*. This memorable day was rounded off with a fantastic banquet and a promising future for German yachting seemed to be assured. Soon after the Kaiser departed onboard *Hohenzollern* for his annual cruise to the Northern Cape.

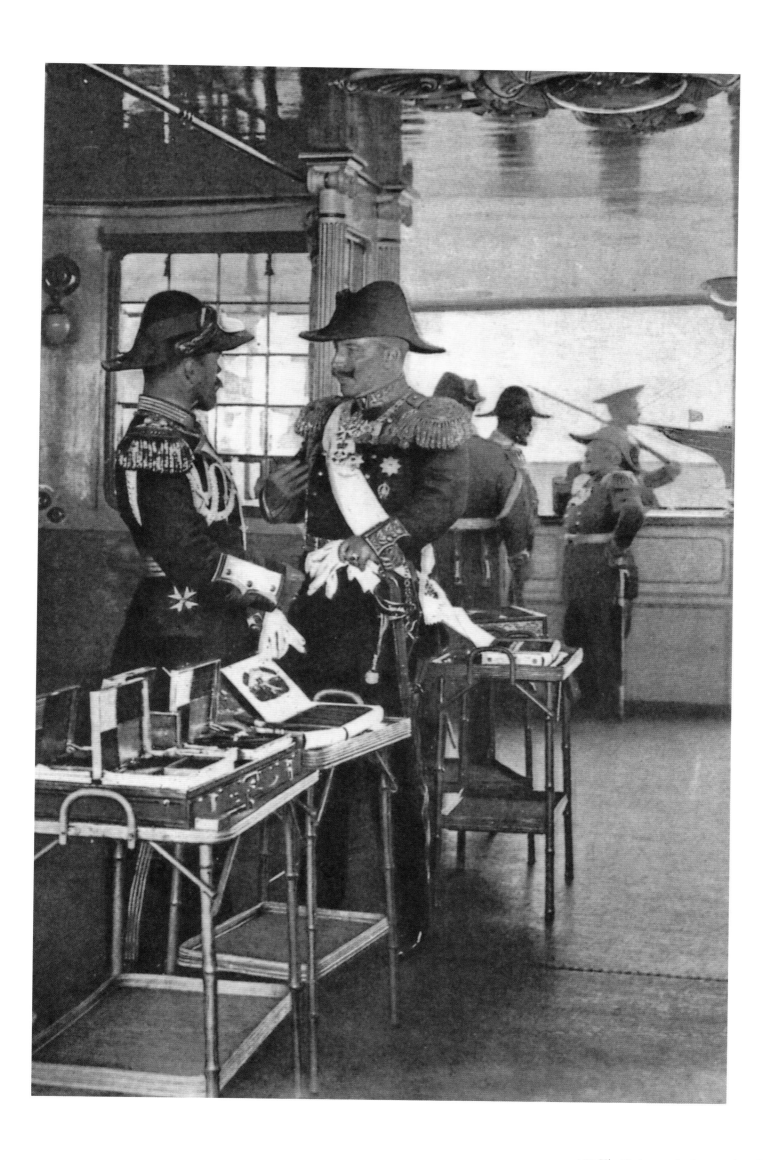

133 *The Kaiser and other royal yachtsmen*

ABOVE
In splendid weather in 1868 the Berliners were able to admire the first races to be held on the Spree surrounded by wooded hills which form a natural amphitheatre.

FACING
Meteor III, a 37-m (121-ft) fast racing schooner, built in the United States in 1903.

FOLLOWING DOUBLE PAGE
The 15-m (50-ft) international gauge boats racing in the Solent. In the lead is the superb Hispania, *designed by Fife for Alfonso XIII, the King of Spain.*

In 1893 Wilhelm II spent 4.5 million marks building *Hohenzollern II*. The imperial yacht measured 127 m (416.7 ft), and her 9,500-horse power gave her a speed of 21.5 knots. She looked more like an enormous destroyer than a pleasure liner despite her luxurious fittings and the imperial eagle painted on her bow. After a cruise in the Baltic Sea in 1894 the Kaiser accompanied by his war ships arrived at Cowes in the middle of Cowes Week. His yacht, the pride of the German sovereign, was 25 m (82 ft) longer than the *Victoria and Albert*. As *Hohenzollern II* passed in front of Osborne House she dipped her flag in salute to the Queen. The Kaiser tried to gain acceptance by British yachtsmen by imitating their behaviour, even though he called his Uncle Edward an 'old peacock'. His gaudy uniform and his concern for protocol, however, made the aristocratic Squadron members smile and remark, 'He is not really a gentleman' – a harsh condemnation. The Kaiser returned slight for slight. When he learnt that Edward VII was on board Thomas Lipton's *Shamrock*, he pretended to be surprised, asking 'How long has my uncle been sailing with his grocer?'

Hohenzollern II returned to Cowes in 1895 making her entry in pounding rain on 5 August. Two days later fine weather returned and the imperial yacht was able to make use of her new equipment to show herself off with

magical effect at night when her rigging was covered with an electric garland of lights and her portholes were illuminated.

The Kaiser frantically set about building yachts and training German crews that would be every bit as good as English ones. His dream was to beat *Britannia*. After *Meteor* he had one of Watson's masterpieces, *Meteor II*, built. She was launched on 13 May 1896 and was 39 m (128 ft) in length.

When *Meteor II* arrived at Kiel, naval vessels were dressed overall and saluted the Emperor's new yacht with a salvo of cannons. The Kaiser went on board and set sail for the *Hohenzollern II* on board which were the Empress and Princess Heinrich.

With the flag of the Hohenzollern eagle flying at her masthead *Meteor II* won all the races in the Thames, overtaking the Royal Yacht *Britannia* on the line. She then ran up to the Clyde escorted by a German naval frigate. The Kaiser's passion for racing led to some dramatic events. During a race of 20-Raters at Cowes *Isolde* was in the lead followed by *Saint* when the class fleet of great yachts caught them up. *Britannia* tried to pass upwind, *Meteor* downwind, and *Isolde* luffed to try to stay clear of *Britannia's* wind but *Saint's* bowsprit got caught up in *Isolde's* back stay and threw her in front of *Meteor's* bow. The German yacht's boom swept across *Isolde's* deck fatally injuring her owner the Baron von Zeidwitz. After this accident the season was cut short and *Britannia* and *Meteor II* didn't take part in any more racing that year.

135 *The Kaiser and other royal yachtsmen*

Despite invitations from the Kaiser and King Edward VII's encouragement, British yachtsmen had little enthusiasm for the Kiel regattas.

In 1897 *Meteor II* ran aground on a sandbank in the Solent. The Emperor was on board and had to suffer the embarrassing spectacle of the crew climbing to the end of the boom and the bowsprit in their attempts to free the schooner. In England and in the Mediterranean the following year, the Kaiser had to admit defeat at the hands of the Duke des Abruzzes who had the advantage of a very favourable partner in his new Watson-designed yacht the *Bona*.

The Kaiser inaugurated Kiel Week,
hoping establish a rival to the Solent regattas. It was all arranged with the utmost propriety in the hope of attracting the most prestigious visitors. There were artillery salvoes, fanfares, parades of goose-stepping guards of honour and interminable banquets. But the starchy receptions were less attractive to the sailors than the open-air parties on the Royal Yacht Squadron lawns and entertaining on

the decks of the yachts moored off Cowes. In the context of this rivalry between Germany and England, the British yachtsmen showed little enthusiasm for racing off German shores in spite of the encouragement from the new King, Edward VII.

The Count of Lonsdale caused a small scandal at Kiel. Lonsdale was nicknamed 'the yellow count' because of his attachment to the colour. His crews were dressed in yellow and his car too was painted yellow. Lonsdale arrived at Kiel onboard his yacht *Finlandia*. He went ashore, handing his bag to the Admiral as if he were just a servant instead of an official welcoming party, and went into the club dressed in striped trousers, yellow waistcoat, a silk shirt with a hunting scarf around his neck, a Panama on his head and a long Havana cigar hanging from his lips.

The 1898 Kiel regatta was a great success, thanks to the participation of several great yachts. *Kommodore* was a newly built German boat but the rest were foreign yachts. *Rainbow*, *Charmian* and *Latona* raced against the Empress's yacht *Iduna*. *Iduna* had been built in Delaware in 1897 as a sailing yacht for the Palmer family. This splendid vessel had crossed the Atlantic, won all the races at Cowes and attracted the interest of the Kaiser who bought it for his wife. *Rainbow* and *Meteor II* raced side by side, each taking the lead in turn. In 1899, *Meteor II* was rerigged as a yawl and the

more favourable handicap allowed her to defeat her opponent *Bona* easily. The same year the German Sailing Federation was formed bringing together the German yacht clubs. In 1902 the Kaiser presented his yacht to the German Navy and placed an order in the United States for *Meteor III*. On 25 February *Hohenzollern II* left Kiel in atrocious weather and travelled via Gibraltar, the Cape Verdi Islands and Saint Thomas, sailing 7,000 miles before arriving in New York where Prince Henry rejoined her. *Meteor III* was a superb cruising schooner. She was launched with all possible pomp in the presence of President Roosevelt and 3,000 invited guests. The bottle of Moët et Chandon champagne was fastened to the end of a 6.1-m (20-ft) silver chain. She was named by no less a personage than the daughter of the American President, Alice Roosevelt, who used a small silver hammer to free the last wedge holding the cradle. The new imperial yacht was close to 50 m (164 ft) in length and the Kaiser himself had planned her layout and fittings.

Following their Sovereign's example wealthy Germans devoted themselves to the joys of yachting. In 1904 a syndicate bought the 40-m (131-ft) Watson designed *Rainbow* which had been built for C. L. Orr Ewing,

a Member of Parliament, and renamed her *Hamburg*. In the same year a German from Kiel had a superb 28.52-m (93.5-ft) schooner built to a Fife design and named her the *Suzanne*. In 1904 King Edward VII was obliged by the demands of diplomacy to attend Kiel Week. He arrived at the entrance to the naval port on 25 June on board *Victoria and Albert*, with the English cruisers *Dido*, *Essex* and *Juno* forming a guard of honour for the royal yacht. The King of England was greeted at the lock by the Kaiser who dressed in an English admiral's uniform with the Order of Bath on his chest and accompanied by his three daughters. The races were notable for the first motor boat competition organised by the German automobile club. The following year Wilhelm II donated a cup for a transatlantic race from Sandy Hook to Lizard Point. Eleven yachts started on 17 May 1905 and it was the *Atlantic* that won the race achieving a record crossing at the same time.

The Coupe de France was held at Kiel in 1907 between *Felca* and Briand de Laubrières' *Armen*. Some prestigious yachts attended the week, yachts such as the King of Spain's *Mouriscot*, Prince Albert of Belgium's *Flandria* and the British *Orion* and *Navahoe*. Yachting in Germany was in full swing with 19 new sailing yachts under construction.

ABOVE
The morning of a happy day's sailing at Kiel in 1912...

FACING PAGE
Kiel Yacht Club.

FOLLOWING DOUBLE PAGE
The inauguration of the Suez Canal in 1869. The Prince of Wales is on board the Royal Yacht Victoria and Albert II.

78 Passage de

...ae de Galles à Port-Saïd.

ABOVE
The imperial yacht
Standart *owned by the*
Russian Tsar Nicholas II
who went cruising on her
every summer.

FACING PAGE
On board Standart,
the Empress's bedroom
(above) and the Tsar's
private sitting room (below).

PRECEDING DOUBLE PAGE
The Russian Sovereign's
visit to France in
September 1901.
The royal family
(Nicholas II and
Alexandra Feodorovna)
leaving on board the
Standart's *steam launch.*

German shipyards set out to rival their English
and Scottish counterparts. The architect Max
Oertz wanted to be on a level with Watson
and Fife and his schooner *Germania* built for
Doctor Krupp von Bohlen was the equal of the
best British yachts in finish and performance.
Her owner had taken the precaution of
ordering a slightly smaller yacht than *Meteor III*
but the *Germania* at 47.21 m (155 ft) in length
and with a half-British, half-German crew
proved herself to be fast. She won such races
as the Kaiser's Cup at Cowes, defeated *Cecily*
and *Carina* and won against *Meteor III* at Kiel.
The Emperor was impressed and ordered his
new yacht from Max Oertz too.
Meteor IV was launched on 28 February 1909
and named by Princess Heinrich of Prussia.
Built of a special steel she proved that German
know-how was equal to that of other countries
and at 48 m (157.5 ft) long she was the greatest
of all the yachts racing at Cowes.

Meteor IV won a name for herself during a
cross-channel race. There was a fresh wind
and the Emperor was on board even though
he suffered from seasickness in bad weather.
His competitors had reefed their sails but the
Emperor's schooner was still fully canvassed
when two hours later the wind strengthened
and the Kaiser's yacht received such a knock-
down that the rudder came out of the water
and the sea poured in through the hatches.
Fortunately, the wind dropped and the crew
managed to regain control of the boat and
slacken the sheets but by then there were
2 m (6.5 ft) of water in the bottom of her hull.
Kiel Week that same year was particularly
grandiose. The races took place between a
guard of honour formed by two lines of
German and British warships. The Coupe
de France was an international competition,
Frederich Kirsten unbeaten till then, raced
against the French yacht *Tilby*, the Danish
Albatros and the Swedish *Elga*, while German
schooners predominated among the great
yachts.
In 1914, George V who had become King
of England in 1910, carried off Wilhelm's
1905 trophy, supposedly made of solid gold
but in reality only base metal covered with
a fine layer of gold. His Highness placed the
Cup on the gunwale and with a single kick
sent it into Kiel harbour.

For many monarchs yachting often wasn't just a
matter of prestige, but something they really enjoyed.

This incident, which signalled the end of an era and imminent worldwide tragedy, was only one of the many signs of the rivalry between the monarchs, which for 30 years had been expressed (among other ways), through the competition between their yachts. The Empress Eugénie's *L'Aigle* and the Austrian Emperor Franz-Joseph's *Greif* both rushed to Port Said for the opening of the Suez Canal in 1869. During the same period the Crown Prince Frederick of Prussia, Prince William-Henry of Holland and Grand Duke Michael of Russia all owned yachts as did Ismaël Pasch the owner of *Mahroussa*. The King of Siam's yacht, the *Maha-Chakrkri* was armed with 15 canons, the King of Portugal owned both *Syrius* and *Amelia*,

and the King of Belgium had *Alberta*. It was all a matter of who owned the largest, most luxurious and fastest yacht of all. Queen Victoria had the *Victoria and Albert III* built purely so that her yacht would be a good as the German Emperor's *Hohenzollern* or the Russian Tsar's *Standart*. The longest and most costly steamers were to be found jostling alongside each other in the Solent, not only those of the British, German, Russian and Belgian monarchs, but also liners belonging to individuals such as John D. Rockfeller, William Vanderbilt and Pierre Lorillard. Lavish receptions were held on board, men in full evening dress, ladies in crinolines and wide-brimmed hats, and there were orchestras, balls, fireworks...

For many monarchs yachting wasn't just a matter of prestige, but something they really enjoyed. Tsar Nicholas II who was married to one of Victoria's granddaughters was affable and reserved, a good father and a good husband. He had inherited the *Pole Star*, which had been launched by his father Alexander III in 1888, but this yacht wasn't good enough for him and he had the 128-m (420 ft) *Standart* built in 1895, which infuriated the Kaiser as she was longer and finer-looking than the *Hohenzollern*. The Tsar's yacht was superb with her gilded bow, black and white painted funnels and sophisticated fittings. Every year Nicholas II, the Tsarina and their five children would go for a two-week cruise in Finland, escorted by torpedo and mail boats and the Tsar would reward the sailors generously with gifts of gold watches. Every evening there would be a concert given by the musicians and then the

family would go the chapel for evening prayers before retiring for the night. During their 1907 cruise the *Standart* went aground, and the Tsar and his family calmly disembarked onto a launch taking with them their icons and jewels. Fortunately, the watertight compartments remained intact and the yacht was able to be refloated. Alfonso XIII, the Spanish king was a skilled sailor. He was one of the first to place an order with Fife for plans for the *Hispania* when the 15-m (50-ft) international gauge series was created in 1907. One of his close friends, the Duke of Medinacelli, had another 15-m (50-ft) yacht, the *Tuiga* built to the same architect's design. In 1910 the Spanish monarch donated a trophy to be contested by French or Spanish built 10-m (32-ft) JIs either in Biarritz or a Spanish port. The Austrian Archduke Charles-Étienne, who sailed on board *Christa* was a naval officer with the

ABOVE
Tsar Nicholas II, the Tsarina, their four daughters and the Tsarevitch Alexis, on board the imperial yacht in 1907.

FACING PAGE
Tsar Nicholas II and family pulling on the oars at Cowes in 1909.

ABOVE AND FACING PAGE
Royal yachting: the Queen of Spain in a sailor suit, Sir Thomas Lipton and, in white, standing, the King of Spain Alfonso XIII, a passionate yachtsman.

FOLLOWING DOUBLE PAGE
The great photographer Gustave Le Gray (1820–1882) immortalised the imperial yacht Reine Hortense *in the port of Le Havre in 1856.*

PAGES 152–153
August 1914. The great British yachts requisitioned by the British Navy became submarine chasers, minesweepers or privateers.

rank of commander. The Prince of Monaco had ordered his 50.4-m (165 ft), three masted, schooner with top-sails in England to a design by Clarke. The Empress Eugénie had a real passion for the sea.

The imperial yacht, *Le Comte d'Eu* was re-named *Reine Hortense* in 1853 and Napoléon III and Empress Eugénie sailed in her across the Channel to visit Queen Victoria in her home at Osborne House. Augustin Normand built the 75-m (246-ft) *Hirondelle* for the Empress in 1869. Her two propellers gave her a speed of over 16 knots during trials. When Empress Eugénie was a widow she spent most of her time travelling on her yacht saying, 'The sea is my element, I would love to live there always'. She cruised to Bergen in 1907 on board *Thistle* and came across some German cruisers waiting for the Kaiser to arrive. Eugénie had some unhappy memories from previous awkward overtures made by Wilhelm II but thought it was too late to turn round by then.

Hohenzollern arrived at 11.30 p.m. to be greeted by an artillery salute. Despite the late hour the Kaiser sent an aide-de-camp to ask if the former Empress would be willing to receive him, and if so at what time and in what dress. Eugénie's reply stipulated, 'At 11 a.m., in civilian dress'.

During his visit the Kaiser expressed a wish to visit Paris but his request was not granted. He would later also tell Tsar Nicholas II of his wish to visit Saint Petersburg, again without success... This reticence among the yachting monarchs was a reflection of the growing tensions among the countries of Europe. The halcyon age of the Edwardian era was drawing to a close.

When, on 28 June 1914, Admiral Muller, having been refused permission to go on board the imperial yacht sailing at Kiel, slipped the cigarette package containing the announcement of the assassination attempt at Sarajevo on to *Meteor's* deck, the Kaiser sighed and said, 'Everything will have to be started all over again'. British yachts were assembled at Cowes for the traditional Cowes Week on 1 August 1914 when Lord Osmond, the Commodore received a message saying, 'The King considers that it is necessary to postpone the regatta'. For a long time.

August 1914, war was declared. For yachting as for the rest of the world
it was the end of the *halcyon Edwardian age*.

Poor and single-handed

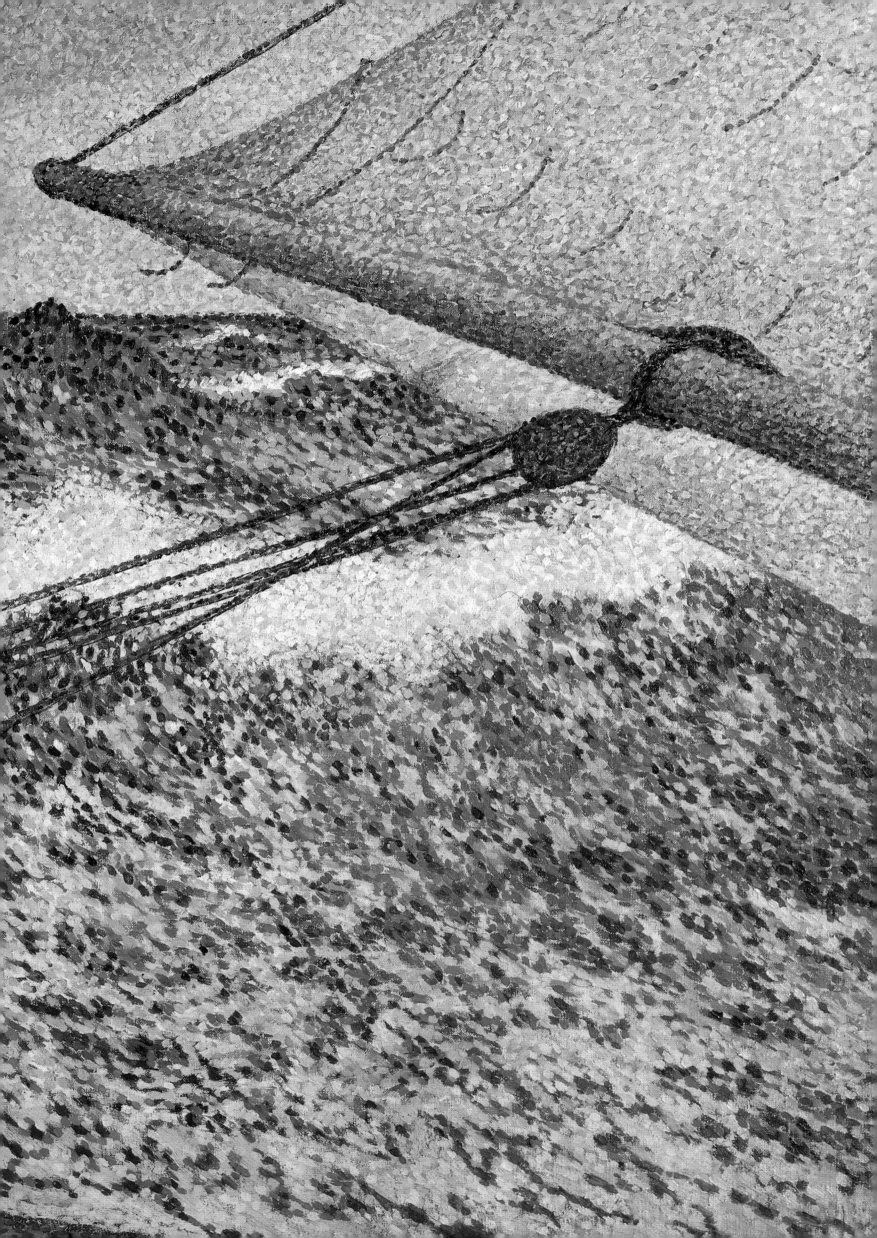

Lone yachtsmen looked down on the Cowes aristocracy and Newport multimillionaires and they distrusted the Solent and Long Island racing yachtsmen. They lived private lives often alone with just their endless love for the sea and sailing for company. They chose to wear fishermen's reefer jackets rather than blazers, white trousers and club ties, and they frequented quayside bars rather than those of the sailing clubs.

Richard Turrell McMullen, British

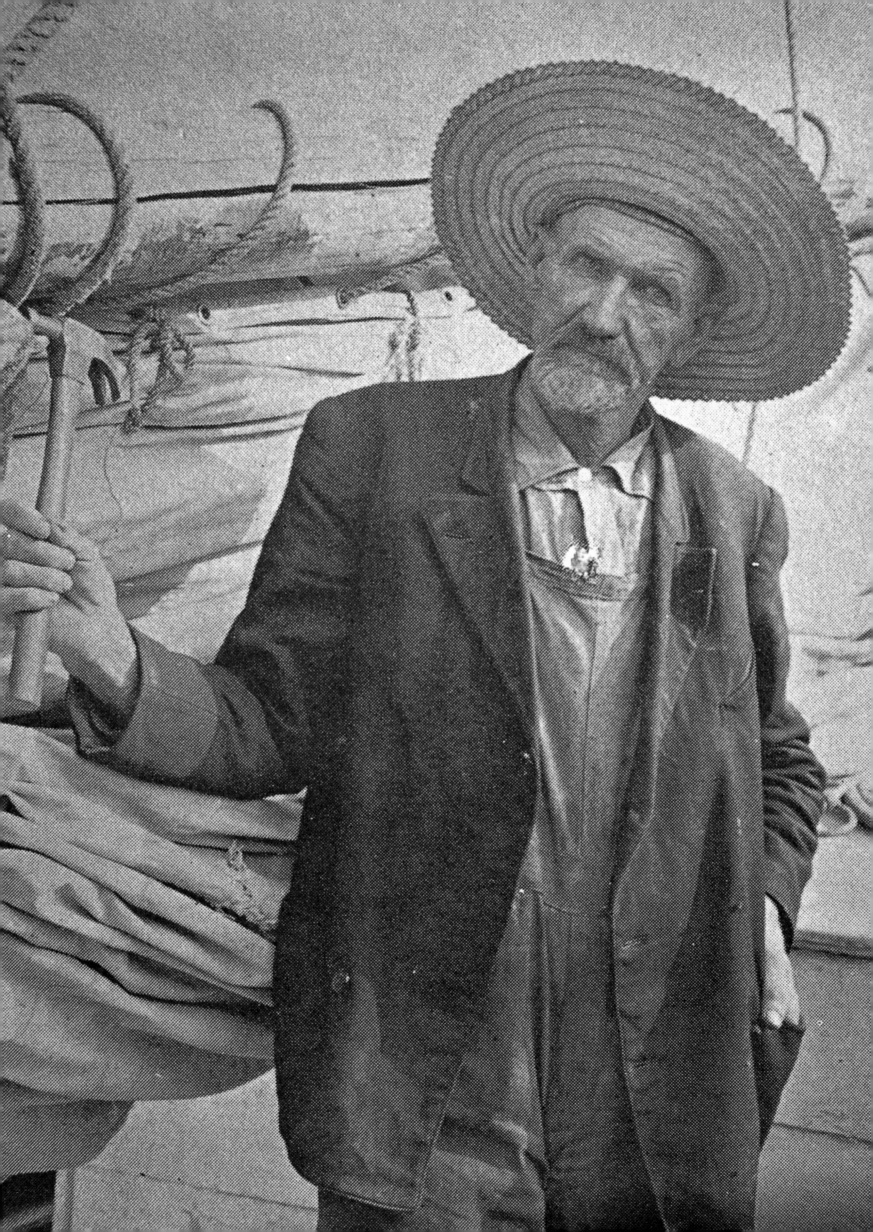

through and through, was one of these. He owned several yachts in succession, the 6.1-m (20-ft) *Leo*, 10-m (32-ft) *Sirius*, and 12.8-m (42-ft) *Orion*. He sailed single-handedly from 1850 onwards, limiting his journeys to the Channel, cruising as far as the Channel Islands and the Isles of Scilly. In 1891, after sailing happily for 41 years, he died of a heart attack while at the helm of his boat on a fine night with a gentle breeze and a new moon. The paper *The Field* wrote 'Mr McMullen was different to all the other sailors we have ever met. We have come across men who were as passionate as he was about the sea, but never any that took such an interest in it. He was not at all interested in yachting or racing'. A lot of lessons were learnt from Richard Turrell McMullen's sailing. It used to be thought that one had to be the son and grandson of seamen to be a sailor. That one had to have been on boats from childhood and to have had practical experience of fishing or navigation in order to acquire the essential skills. It was also believed that a landlubber wouldn't have either the necessary strength or knowledge handed down through the combined skills of several generations. In his book, *Down Channel*, Richard Turrell McMullen wrote that he had learnt more in a few months of sailing alone than he would have from years of sailing with

a professional. He proved through experience that it is the coast that is dangerous, and that safety is to be found at sea. He proved that a well-built small yacht in skilled hands is as safe as a large yacht.

Around 1860 another yachtsman E. E. Middleton sailed single-handedly around the British Isles, and as he arrived back where he had started, he came to the conclusion that the earth was flat which he then confirmed by an exchange of letters with the Astronomer Royal at Greenwich. Edward Knight another pioneer of single-handed sailing, who was born in 1852, explained that it wasn't necessary to be wealthy and that one could go sailing for very little cost on a converted lifeboat, a former fishing-boat or by buying a low-priced second-hand yacht. Another enthusiastic sailor was C. C. Lyon, the headmaster of Oxford Preparatory School. He was a robust character, with a ruddy face surrounded by white hair, which he rarely had cut and which curled over his ears. He sailed to the north of Scotland, to the Hebrides, the Orkneys, Shetland and round the Northern Cape, taking advantage of the Easter and summer school holidays to sail and sail and sail....

In 1870, the American, John Buckley, accompanied by Primoraz, an Austrian, made the first transatlantic crossing from east to west on

ABOVE
Spray, the 11.2-m (36.7-ft), 100-year-old oyster smack rebuilt by Slocum was the first yacht to sail around the world single-handed.

FACING PAGE
'No sailor has ever done what I have achieved,' boasted Captain Slocum on his return.

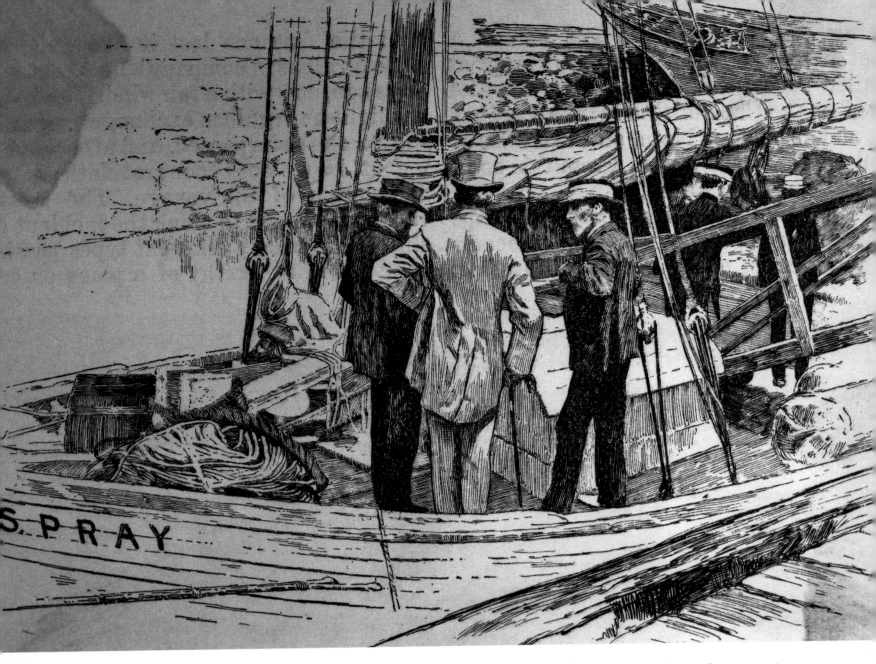

During Slocum's stop in South Africa
he was told by *President Kruger*,
who believed the earth was flat that,
'You have not travelled around the world
but on the world'.

ABOVE
*Slocum received Sir Alfred
Milner and Colonel
Saunderson on board.
Wherever he went Slocum,
who was known through
the articles he sent to the
American papers, received
an enthusiastic welcome.*

FACING PAGE
Spray *at Sydney. Captain
Slocum was forced to
arrange visits to his boat
to raise money to pay for
his provisions before he
could continue his journey.*

board a converted lifeboat, the *City of Ragusa*.
In 1876 the American, Alfred Johnson, a former
fisherman was the first to complete a single-
handed ocean crossing, sailing from Nova
Scotia to Wales on his 5-m (16.5-ft) fishing
boat *Centennial*. However, it wasn't until 1880
that a club specifically for cruising was formed.
On an autumn evening several sailors met in
Arthur Underhill's room in Lincoln's Inn and set
up the Cruising Club, which would later be
given the title of Royal Cruising Club, with
Arthur Underhill as its president, a post he
would hold for half a century. From 1882, the
association circulated its members' cruising
tales, leading to the regular publication of the
Cruising Club Journal. The Cruising Association
and the Clyde Yacht Club were founded in
1908. In 1910 Claud Worth's great classic of
maritime literature *Yacht Cruising* was
published. 'The author wrote that the most
perfect expression of the sport for those who

love the sea is to go sailing on the open sea in
one's own boat, not running any unnecessary
risks or without fear of bad weather, but having
confidence in one's own knowledge and ability
to face whatever may happen'.

At the end of the nineteenth century
an exceptional American, Joshua Slocum,
best exemplified the joy to be found in
crossing oceans by completing the first
single-handed world tour. He had been
born in Nova Scotia in 1844 to a poor
family with 11 children and gained his
knowledge of the sea with the other
young tearaways of Fundy Bay. He joined
a fishing boat at 14, worked his way up
to be promoted to lieutenant at 18 and
then became captain. He was slim and tall,
with fine features, bright eyes and was very
agile. He became an American national and
at 25 commanded a coastal schooner, then
a three-master. During a stop over in Sydney
he met and married Virginia, the daughter
of an Indian mother, who was the great love
of his life and who travelled with him on his
ships. At Manilla he worked in partnership
with a boatyard as he was a skilled boat
builder, received a 90-ton schooner, the
Pato, as payment and then used her to trade
profitably along the coast.

"As for myself the wonderful sea charmed me from the first." Joshua Slocum

The *Spray*

PRECEDING DOUBLE PAGE
Slocum's fantastic adventure led several yachtsmen to build copies of his famous Spray, as shown here.

ABOVE
A picture of Spray signed by Slocum. The yawl could hold her heading at any speed with the helm fixed.

His seamanship and boat-handling skills were superb. He arrived in Hong Kong one day when the harbour was crowded with British warships and there were no tugs available. Joshua Slocum wasn't deterred. He simply sailed into the port, skirting around the other ships without touching any of them, and anchored in the middle of the fleet.

But the carefree days were coming to an end as increasing competition from steam-driven boats made life difficult for sailing boats. Slocum acquired a small three-masted boat the *Aquidnecq* and took cargoes to Brazil always accompanied by his wife and their children who were born on board. Virginia was 34 when she died in Rio de la Plata worn out by repeated pregnancies. Joshua was distraught but he couldn't live alone. His contemporaries told of his 'warm and affectionate temperament, his strong sexuality and his need for intimacy'. Less than two years after Virginia's death he married Henrietta, known as Hettie, a pretty cousin who at

24 years old was 18 years younger than him. He set off on his journeys to South America again on board *Aquidnecq* but his second wife didn't love the sea in the same way as his first had. Besides, his crew were real bandits and Slocum had to shoot and kill one of them to quell a mutiny. Then, caught by contrary winds and currents, *Aquidnecq* was blown ashore and lost. The crew was sent home but Slocum bolstered by his experience as the boss of a boatyard, built a 10.67-m (35-ft) launch which he called *Libertad*, and took Hettie and the children home on her in a 8,800-km (5,500-mile) voyage lasting 53 days. Slocum, who had left school when he was very young, wrote a book of his exploits and paid for it to be published but it wasn't very successful. He couldn't find any more cargoes; White Star offered him a command but he refused saying 'I've been sailing since I was 14. If I were to accept your offer I would have to get used to steamboats and I don't like them'. The family had little money so had to live with relatives and Joshua and Hettie's relationship suffered. The *Libertad* adventure had put Hettie off sailing forever and she refused to go on board a boat again. A friend of Joshua's who was a whaling captain told him, 'come to Fairhaven and I will give you a boat. She does need some work doing on her though'. The boat had been built a hundred years previously and was almost totally rotten having been left in a field for seven years. She was called *Spray*, was 11.2 m (36.7 ft) long and 3.2 m (10.5 ft) wide but only drew 1.27 m (5.3 ft). She wasn't particularly appealing but Slocum had no choice and he re-built her piece by piece over a period of 13 months. Once he had finished the work he tried fishing but without success, but tempted by the seaworthiness and handling of the boat he decided to sail her round the world. He asked Hettie to go with him but she refused, saying 'I have already done that, so he went on his own. He said, 'I will send my reports to a newspaper syndicate in the hope that I have something interesting to tell'. The *Boston Globe* commenting on this extraordinary plan described their hero as follows: 'Captain Slocum is an original old sea dog. He is 1.78 m (6 ft) tall, weighs 66 kilos (148 lb) and is as lively as a cat and agile as a monkey'.

Slocum was 51 when he got under way on 2 July 1895. He had spent his last dollar fitting out and provisioning his boat. His chronometer needed repairing but he didn't have the $15 to pay the watchmaker so he made do with a $1.5 clock that he got for $1 as the dial was cracked. His provisions were limited to some potatoes, dried cod and ship's biscuits. He was both worried and happy, saying 'I have this new feeling of being alone. During those first days at sea I was frightened'. He had been told that if he stayed quiet for too long he would lose the use of his voice so he shouted out orders which he then carried out himself having no crew to do it for him. For company he would sing sea shanties. He discovered that the former oyster boat had an amazing ability to hold its course whatever its speed once the helm was fixed. 'I only needed a little time to find the right setting for the helm that would allow me to stay on course. Once I had done that I fixed the helm in position. The ease with which *Spray* kept her course downwind for weeks on end was a constant source of amazement'.

After a stop in the Azores, Slocum was given a hero's welcome in Gibraltar. His original plan had been to travel through the Suez Canal but he was warned against it by British officials because of the threat of piracy, so he went through the Magellan Straits instead. However, he was chased by North Africans off the Barbary Coast. He strengthened sail in a freshening wind but a felucca was still gaining on him when *Spray's* boom broke. The main sail needed to be struck but the pirates would have caught up with him by the time the repairs had been done. Slocum turned round, a gun in his hand, but the felucca had lost her mast and the Berbers' boat was crippled! The sailor had overcome his feeling of solitude. He didn't worry about making any visits ashore but arrived at Pernambuco after 40 days at sea. He boasted 'No sailor has ever achieved what I have done'. The articles he sent to the American papers spread the news of his journey. At Montevideo his double crossing was greeted with enthusiasm and all the boats sounded their whistles in salute. He continued his journey south. 'When I was working with the sails and the rigging, I was only thinking about the next thing. It was only when I was moored in lonely and desolate places that I felt fear overcoming me'.

In February 1896, Spray rounded Cape Virgin and sailed into the difficult Magellan Straits with their strong currents, powerful winds and the aggressive, thieving inhabitants of Tierra del Fuego. At Punta Arenas an old captain gave him a sack of upholstery tacks with the recommendation, 'be careful not to walk on them yourself'.

He went back to sea and found himself absolutely alone in the superb surroundings of the Straits 'with scarcely a bird in sight' in celebration of his 52nd birthday. Sailing alone meant it was impossible to keep the permanent watch that was necessary as natives posed a threat to the boat. Ingeniously Slocum made two dummies, stood one by the forward hatch and the other looking as though it was coming out of the aft cabin, which gave the illusion of a three-man crew. In the evenings he scattered tacks over the deck and was woken up by the cries of bare footed Alakalufs or Yaghans who had thought it would be easy to take control of the cutter. They finished up by jumping into

their dinghies or even the water 'doubtless to cool down' according to Slocum, who would fire a few shoots just to confirm that he was keeping watch. Slocum had a sense of humour. At one anchorage he laid claim to a small island that wasn't marked on the chart and planted a sign saying, 'Keep off the grass'. After a journey made difficult by westerly winds, he arrived in the Pacific but a north-westerly wind forced him run downwind, trailing anchor ropes to slow *Spray* down. Slocum, displaying extraordinary stamina stayed at the helm for 30 hours. The boat behaved magnificently. 'My confidence in her extraordinary nautical qualities will last forever'. On the second night there were shoals all around the boat. Slocum, in great danger had to pull away from the hazardous coast and return to the Magellan Straits through the Cockburn Channel, and then had to repeat the journey! He rounded Pilar Point for the second time and sailed out into the open sea, 'small waves, friendly waves knocked gently on *Spray's* hull telling long tales that I could see my boat was pleased to hear'. Having at last reached the Pacific, Slocum visited the Juan Fernandez Islands, then put out to sea again. He didn't stop at Tahiti, or at Tuamotu. He passed within sight of Fatu-Hiva, the most southern of the Marquesa Islands, but

ABOVE
The American, Harry Pidgeon, on his Seabird Islander was the second single-handed round-the-world sailor. After his journey around the world he received the most prestigious award for yachtsmen, the Blue Water Medal.

FACING PAGE
*Henry Pidgeon at the stern
of his yawl* Islander.

FOLLOWING DOUBLE PAGE
*At the end of his round-
the-world trip on* Firecrest
*in 1932, Alain Gerbault,
the first French round-
the-world, single-handed
sailor was welcomed at
Le Havre with the Légion
d'honneur. But war had
already brought the halcyon
Edwardian age to a close...*

after 43 days at sea, which had gone by very
pleasantly, he decided to carry on. Slocum was
happy and he no longer found the solitude
wearing.
'Without having sampled it for themselves, no
one can have any idea of the joy to be found in
sailing freely on the vast oceans. Wherever my
boat and I were to be found the days passed by
easily and happily'. The flying fish that he ate
for his breakfast brought some variety to the
monotony of his diet. 'I was gifted with a truly
voracious appetite. This was the life. I was
completely happy with my cook for the whole
journey and he found nothing in me to
complain about either'. He read a lot, mended
his clothes and ate his meals in peace. 'Nothing
more restful and easy than my journey in the
trade winds could be imagined'. After 72 days
at sea he arrived at Samoa, 'during all that time
I never once suffered from loneliness'.
Slocum visited Stevenson's widow, then carried
on to Australia through some terrible weather,
but 'the *Spray* took to it like a duck to water,
and her canvas and deck remained completely
dry'. He received a warm welcome in Sydney
and became a guide to earn some money,
charging 6 pence to visit his boat. A journalist
on the *Sydney Morning Herald* wrote, 'Captain
Slocum's bold exploits are unique and it is very
unlikely that they will often be imitated'.

Slocum navigated faultlessly using
only a watch with a cracked face, which was
also missing its hour hand, as his chronometer.
Landing on the Cocos Keeling atoll with its
base under water was tricky. 'I climbed aloft,
stopping halfway, and saw the coconut palms
straight ahead looking as though they were
coming out of the water. I was expecting to
see it but it hit me like an electric shock.
I slid back down the mast, seized by the most
strange emotion and, sitting on the deck let
myself go, incapable of resisting the feelings
that were coursing through me'. The lone sailor
could be proud of his navigation. 'My dead
reckoning had been more accurate than on
any of my previous boats, however skilled
the officers were who had been doing it.
By reading through the log books of former
sailors, I believe that they were far from making
as correct landfalls as the *Spray* using their
methods'. After briefly stopping at Rodigues
Island and Mauritius, where he was received
like royalty, Slocum arrived in Natal to the
following greeting in the local paper. 'The skill
with which Captain Slocum sailed his boat
amongst the ships was a real treat for all
onlookers'. At the Cape he met President
Kruger who told him, 'you have not travelled
around the world but on the world,' for the
statesman still believed that the earth was flat,
and three Boers had prepared a report to
support his point of view.
Off the West Indies, the battleship *Oregon*
informed Slocum that the United States and
Latin America were at war and the sailor,

> *'Without having sampled it for themselves,
> no one can have any idea of the joy to be found
> in sailing freely on the vast oceans.'*
> Joshua Slocum

ABOVE
*The Argentinian, Vito
Dumas, was the first to
sail around the world by
the three southern capes.*

FACING PAGE
*Vito Dumas' companion the
Legh II, a 9.55-m (31-ft)
ketch with a Norwegian
stern designed by the
Argentinian architect
Manuel Campos.*

always one for a joke, signalled this message with his flags 'Let's stay together for our mutual protection'. On 3 July 1898 he moored *Spray* to the post he had driven in for her launch. The boat hadn't so much as a drop of water in her and Slocum himself seemed to be ten years younger. He wrote and published an account of his trip around the world, saying that on balance, 'I found what I was looking for, and a few more things that I wasn't expecting, through sailing'. He playfully said, 'I only came across happy circumstances, although my adventures were completely prosaic and devoid of the picturesque'. He was bold enough to say 'I don't think that my record can be beaten, even by strength of courage, endurance and tenacity. I know that it is difficult to do any better'. Even while admiring his exploits many yachtsmen thought that the *Spray* was the worst boat that one could imagine for taking out on the open sea. L. Francis Herreshoff, the son of the 'Bristol Sorcerer' commented 'I have the greatest admiration for Captain Slocum's skill in going around the world in such a terrible boat'.

Slocum bought a little farm in the middle of Martha's Vineyard for $305 and settled down to life with Hettie, a life which was frequently interrupted by Slocum's sailing expeditions. He met Archibald Roosevelt in Oyster Bay. The president's son went sailing with him on *Spray* and invited the ageing sailor to Sagamore Hill, Theodore Roosevelt's summer 'White House'. He praised Slocum and said, 'I fully sympathise with the joyful feelings that the immensity and solitude of the oceans inspire in you'. But old age was approaching and the captain, previously so meticulous, was neglecting his boat.

In 1905 and then every autumn, Slocum would leave to spend the winters in the sun of the West Indies or the Bahamas. When he returned to New York in 1908 he seemed tired, his boat very dirty and the rigging slack with dirty ropes. When he was 65, Joshua Slocum decided to sail over to the Orinoco and he set out for the open sea on 14 November 1909. *Spray* and Joshua Slocum would never be seen again.

Slocum's was the forerunner of numerous single-handed round the world voyages. In the 1920s, the Americans Thommy Drake and Harry Pidgeon followed in his footsteps. In 1932 it was the turn of the first Frenchman, Alain Gerbault, and then an Argentinian, Vito Dumas, sailed around the world by the three southern capes in 1942–43. Over the years to come many others would clearly prove that it is possible to find happiness on the oceans without being a monarch, a member of the aristocracy or a multimillionaire.

Photographic credits

lt: left; rt: right; h: high; lo: low;
m: middle; rr: rights reserved

Cover: © Mitchell Library, Glasgow
Back of cover: © Hulton Archives
Endpapers and p. 16: © J. M. Barrault/Sea & See
pp. 4–5 and p. 16: © Beken of Cowes
pp. 6–7 and p. 16: © Beken of Cowes
pp. 8–9 and pp. 16–17: © Hulton Archives
pp. 10–11 and p. 17: © RMN – Gérard Blot,
   ADAGP 2002
pp. 12–13 and p. 17: © Photothèque
   Hachette-Livre
p. 14 and p. 17: © Mitchell Library, Glasgow
pp. 18–19: © Bridgeman Giraudon
p. 20: © DR
p. 22 h: © DR (illustration of Louis Vallet
   in Philippe Daryl, *Le Yacht*)
p. 22 lo: © DR (illustration of Louis Vallet
   in Philippe Daryl, *Le Yacht*)
p. 23 h: © Mitchell Library
p. 23 lo: © Getty/Hulton Archive
pp. 24–25: © Bridgeman Giraudon
p. 24 lo: © Bridgeman Giraudon
p. 26 h: © Bridgeman Giraudon
p. 26 lo: © Collection François Chevalier
   & Jacques Taglang
p.27: © Bridgeman Giraudon
pp. 28–29, 30, 31: © Collection François
   Chevalier & Jacques Taglang
p. 32: © Beken of Cowes
p. 33 h, and m, lo: © Collection François
   Chevalier & Jacques Taglang
pp. 34–35: © L'Illustration/Keystone
p. 36 h: © Photothèque Hachette-Livre
p. 36 lo: © Collection François Chevalier
   & Jacques Taglang
p. 37: © Collection François Chevalier
   & Jacques Taglang
pp. 38–39: © Bridgeman Giraudon
   ADAGP 2002
p. 40: © Hulton Archive
p. 41: © Mitchell Library, Glasgow
p. 43 h and lo: © Beken of Cowes
p. 44: © Collection François Chevalier
   & Jacques Taglang
p. 45: © Mitchell Library, Glasgow
pp. 46–47: © Wadsworth Atheneum Museum of
   Art, Hartford, CT. The Ella Gallup Sumner and
   Mary Catlin Sumner Collection Fund.
p. 49: © Bridgeman Giraudon
p. 50: © Mystic Seaport Museum, Connecticut
p. 51: © Henry G. Peabody, Droit collection,
   Library of Congress
p. 52: © Mystic Seaport Museum, Connecticut
p. 53 h: © Brown Brothers, Sterling,
   Pennsylvania
p. 53 lo: © Marc P. G Berthier/Collection
   François Chevalier & Jacques Taglang.
p. 54: © L'Illustration/Keystone
p. 55: © Collection François Chevalier
   & Jacques Taglang
pp. 56–57: © Courtesy of The Preservation
   Society of Newport County
p. 58: © Nathaniel L. Stebbins, 1899.
   Courtesy of the Society for the Preservation
   of New England Antiquities.
p. 59: © Beken of Cowes

p. 60 h: © Collection François Chevalier
   & Jacques Taglang
p. 60 lo: © Photothèque Hachette-Livre
p. 61: © Collection François Chevalier
   & Jacques Taglang
pp. 62–63: © Collection François
   Chevalier & Jacques Taglang
p. 63 h: © Statens Sjohistoriska Museum,
   Stockholm
p. 63 lo: © Mystic Seaport, Rosenfeld
   Collection, Mystic, CT
pp. 64–65: © Beken of Cowes
p. 66 h: © Beken of Cowes
p. 66 lo: © Mystic Seaport, Mystic, CT
p. 67: © Herreshoff Marine Museum,
   Rhode Island
p. 68: © Bettmann/Corbis
p. 69: © Herreshoff Marine Museum,
   Rhode Island
pp. 70–71: © Mystic Seaport, Rosenfeld
   Collection, Mystic, CT
pp. 72–73: © Beken of Cowes
p. 74: © Musée de la Marine
p. 75: © François Chevalier & Jacques Taglang
pp. 76–77: © Association L'Hirondelle de la
   Manche (private collection)
p. 78: © Bridgeman/Giraudon (special
   collection)
p. 80: © Société des Régates du Havre.
p. 81 h and lo: © Collection François Chevalier
   & Jacques Taglang
p. 82 h: © Roger-Viollet
p. 82 lo: © Société des Régates du Havre
p. 83: © Bridgeman/Giraudon, National Gallery
   of Victoria, Melbourne, Australia
pp. 84–85: © Musée national de la Marine/
   P. Dantec – D. R.
p. 86: © Roger-Viollet
p. 87 h: © Collection. François Chevalier
   & Jacques Taglang
p. 87 lo: © Roger-Viollet
p. 88 h: © Bridgeman/Giraudon, (special
   collection)
p. 88 lo: © L'Illustration/Keystone
p. 89: © Collection François Chevalier
   & Jacques Taglang
pp. 90–91: © Bridgeman/Giraudon,
   Gavin Graham Gallery, London
p. 92: © Collection François Chevalier
   & Jacques Taglang
p. 93: © AKG Paris, Erich Lessing
pp. 94–95: © Bridgeman/Giraudon,
   ADAGP 2002
p. 96 h and lo: © Collection François Chevalier
   & Jacques Taglang
p. 97: © RMN, Musée d'Orsay/Gérard Blot
pp. 98–99: © Roger-Viollet
p. 100: © Photothèque Hachette-Livre
p. 101: © Collection François Chevalier
   & Jacques Taglang
p. 102 h and lo: © Collection François
   Chevalier & Jacques Taglang
p. 103: © Collection François Chevalier
   & Jacques Taglang
p. 104: © Collection François Chevalier
   & Jacques Taglang
p. 105: © RMN, Musée d'Orsay/
   Gérard Blot

pp. 106–107: © RMN, Musée d'Orsay/
   Hervé Lewandovski
pp. 108–109: © Bridgeman/Giraudon,
   The Royal Cornwall Museum, Truro
p. 111: © DR
p. 112: © Underwood & Underwood/Corbis
p. 113: © Photothèque Hachette-Livre
p. 114 h and lo: © Collection Monique Prigent
p. 115: © Photothèque Hachette-Livre
pp. 116–117: © Beken of Cowes
pp. 118–119: © L'Illustration/Keystone
p. 120 h and lt: © Collection François Chevalier
   & Jacques Taglang
p. 121 h: © Mitchell Library, Glasgow
p. 121 lo: © L'Illustration/Keystone
pp. 122–123: © L'Illustration/Keystone
pp. 124–125: © Ullstein/Bilderdienst
p. 126: © Ullstein/Bilderdienst
p. 128: © Hulton Archive/Getty
p. 129: © L'Illustration/Keystone
p. 130: © Ullstein/Bilderdienst
p. 131: © AKG, Paris
p. 132: © Beken of Cowes
p. 133: © L'Illustration/Keystone
p. 134: © AKG, Paris
p. 135: © AKG, Paris
pp. 136–137: © Beken of Cowes
p. 138: © Hulton-Deutsch Collection/
   CORBIS
p. 139: © Hulton Archive/Getty
pp. 140–141: © Hulton Archive/Getty
pp. 142–143: © L'Illustration/Keystone
pp. 144: © L'Illustration/Keystone
p. 145 h and lo: © L'Illustration/Keystone
p. 146: © Mary Evans Picture Library
p. 147: © Harlingue/Roger-Viollet
p. 148: © Mitchell Library, Glasgow
p. 149: © Mitchell library, Glasgow
pp. 150–151: © Corbis/Philip de Bay
pp. 152–153: © Beken of Cowes
pp. 154–155: © RMN, — Jean Schormans,
   ADAGP 2002
p. 157: © Collection François Chevalier
   & Jacques Taglang
p. 158: © Collection François Chevalier
   & Jacques Taglang
p. 159: © Collection François Chevalier
   & Jacques Taglang
p. 160: © Bettmann/Corbis
p. 161: © D. Allisy/Sea & See
p. 162–163: © D. Allisy/Sea & See
p. 164: © D. Allisy/Sea & See
p. 165: © Keystone
pp. 166–167: © Keystone
p. 168: © Keystone
p. 169 h lo: © Keystone
p. 170: © Allisy/Sea & See
p. 171: © Allisy/Sea & See

Bibliography

Jean-Michel Barrault, *Les Grandes Heures du Yachting*, Robert Laffont
Beken, *America's Cup*, Harvill Press
Beken, *Gloire de la Voile*, Arthaud
Beken, *Hundred Years of Sail*, Harvill Press
Beken, *Sailing Thoroughbreds*, Harvill Press
Daniel Charles, *Les Chasseurs de Future*, EMOM
Daniel Charles, *Histoire du Yachting*, Arthaud
Daniel Charles, *Le Mystère Caillebotte*, Glénat
Daniel Charles, *Le Yachting*, EMOM
François Chevalier et Jacques Taglang, *Velox*
Philippe Daryl, *Le Yacht*
Ian Dear, *Enterprise to Endeavour: J-class Yachts*, Adlard Coles
David Glenn, *Nautical Style*, Scriptum
Jack Grout, *C'était au Temps des Yachtsmen*, Voiles/Gallimard
Peter Heaton, *History of Yachting in Pictures*, T Stacey
Ed Holm *Yachting's Golden Age, 1880-1905: 1880-1905* Alfred Knopf
John Illingworth, *La Coupe de l'America*, Robert Laffont
Klaus Kramer, *Vom Gondelcorso zum Ocean-Race*, Klaus Kramer Verlag
Gilles Martin-Raget, *Yachts Classiques*, Éditions du Chêne
Françoise de Maulde, *Sir Thomas Lipton*, Gallimard
Jean Merrien, *Les Navigateurs Solitaires*, Denoël
Douglas Phillips-Birt, *The History of Yachting*, Elm Tree books
Erwan Quémére et François-Jean Dahen, *À Bord des plus Beaux Voiliers du Monde*, Gallimard
Joshua Slocum, *Sailing Alone Around the World*, Adlard Coles
W. Teller, *Slocum Homme de Mer*, Chiron
G.P. Thierry, *À Travers un Siècle de Yachting à Voile*, EMOM
G.P. Thierry, *Le Yachting de Course*, EMOM
A.B.C. Whipple et les Rédacteurs des Éditions Time-Life, *Les Yachts de Luxe*, Time Life

Periodicals
Le Yacht
Bulletin du Yacht Club de France

Index

EDITOR
Nathalie Bailleux

ARTISTIC EDITOR
Sabine Houplain

GRAPHIC DESIGN AND PRODUCTION
Rachida Zerroudi

ILLUSTRATIONS
Stéphanie Aulestia

PRODUCTION
Nicole Thiériot-Pichon and Mathilde Allier

The editor would like to thank the Royal Yacht Squadron (Cowes) for the photograph on page 20
as well as Philippe Valetoux and Anne de Bagneaux-Savatier of the SRH du Havre
for their invaluable help with illustration research. The editor would also like to thank all those
at the Éditions du Chêne who were involved in the preparation of this book, especially
Anne Cribier, Anne-Sophie Guirlet, Alice Harang, Stéphanie Mastronicola and François Huertas.

PHOTOENGRAVING
Chromostyle – Tours

First published by Editions du Chêne, an imprint of Hachette-Livre
43 Quai de Grenelle, Paris 75905, Cedex 15, France
© 2002, Editions du Chêne – Hachette Livre

Under the title *La Belle Epoque du Yachting*
All rights reserved

Language translation produced by Translate-A-Book, Oxford

This edition published by Hachette Illustrated UK, Octopus Publishing Group Ltd.,
2–4 Heron Quays, London, E14 4JP
English Translation © 2004, Octopus Publishing Group Ltd., London

Printed in Italy by Editoriale Lloyd
ISBN-13: 978-1-84430-080-8
ISBN-10: 1 84430 080 3